THE OTHER SI

To Gwyneth —
Clive of India,

I hope this is
of real use!!
God Bless,
Tal Brooke

The Other Side of DEATH

DOES DEATH SEAL YOUR DESTINY?

TAL BROOKE

Tyndale House Publishers, Inc.
Wheaton, Illinois

SCRIPTURE REFERENCES IN THIS BOOK ARE
QUOTED FROM THE KING JAMES VERSION OF THE
BIBLE UNLESS OTHERWISE INDICATED.
OTHER VERSIONS OF THE BIBLE ARE
IDENTIFIED AS FOLLOWS:

BERKELEY	BERKELEY VERSION
REVISED BERKELEY	REVISED BERKELEY VERSION
NASB	NEW AMERICAN STANDARD BIBLE
PHILLIPS	THE NEW TESTAMENT IN MODERN ENGLISH
RSV	REVISED STANDARD VERSION
TEV	TODAY'S ENGLISH VERSION

LIBRARY OF CONGRESS CATALOG CARD NUMBER 78-66202
ISBN 0-8423-4759-3, PAPER

COPYRIGHT © 1979 BY TAL BROOKE. ALL RIGHTS RESERVED.
FIRST PRINTING, MAY 1979.
PRINTED IN THE UNITED STATES OF AMERICA.

ACKNOWLEDGMENTS

Invariably there is a special circle of people whose heart support and encouragement become almost an organic part of a project of this scope. So from my heart let me express my gratitude to the Hedrick clan, Julia Neal, the Wheelers, Pettys, Jarvises, Metcalfs, Rich Ruch, and the men on Shepherds Hill: John Owen, a man who has traveled the globe with me, Tony Morton, and Preston Campbell. I am further grateful to encouragement from Al Martin, Hal Lindsey, and Joni Eareckson.

Furthermore, I deeply appreciate the efforts of two close friends in helping with this book: the careful editing and the contributions in the area of Western philosophy by Robert Schlagal, now a Ph.D. candidate in English at the University of Virginia, and the generosity of Brooks Alexander, director of the Spiritual Counterfeits Project.

I am eternally indebted to two people who helped me break the seal of death almost ten years ago in the heart of south India: Ivan and Winonna Carroll, who themselves had spent thirty-five years in India and unceasingly pursued me down the highways of desolation to show me the truth of what really lay at the other side of death.

Finally, may this book in some way acknowledge my gratitude to my parents, Edgar and Frances Brooke, and serve to assure them of eternal hope after death.

CONTENTS

Foreword 9

SECTION ONE: THE ISSUE 13
1. Sudden Death 15
2. The New Breakthrough 18
3. Finding a Definition for Death 26

**SECTION TWO: EXPERIENCES OF THE BEYOND—
PSYCHICS, MEDIUMS, AND THE OCCULT 31**
4. The Psychic Death Experience 33
5. Beings of Light or False
   Angels of Light? 50

**SECTION THREE: DEATH IN THE EAST—
YOGIS, MYSTICS, AND MYSTERY RELIGIONS 65**
6. The Ancient Tradition: Its
   Heart and Essence 67
7. Dying in India: The Symptoms
   of the Ancient Tradition 74
8. Death in Babylon 85

**SECTION FOUR: DEATH IN THE WEST—
PHILOSOPHY, SCIENCE, AND COSMIC HUMANISM 97**
9. The Present Mood 99
10. The Death of God 104

SECTION FIVE: THE REVELATION OF GOD 113
11. The Eternal Word 115
12. The Eternal Day 126

Conclusion 144

APPENDIXES 149
1. The West: The Great Revolt 151
2. The West: The Point of No Return 159
3. Old Testament Predictions Which
   Were Literally Fulfilled in Christ 169

FOREWORD

In the past few years, the mystery of death has apparently been solved by a new category of "scientific breakthroughs" in the realm of advanced resuscitation methods in medical technology. Those declared "clinically dead" have apparently come back with a wide range of reports about the afterlife. Now a number of researchers have appeared on the scene to interpret the ultimate meaning of these reports. And we find that each researcher has peered into this garbled field of death reports to prove, at face value, his own schema of afterlife. And yet none of them seems to see that the data they have grasped to prove their beliefs—testimonies of experience—can, like Proteus, change in an instant, turn, and ultimately destroy the faith that sought to use it. The argument in essence amounts to this: If you believe in one report you are forced to believe them all, and then you are left to tabulate them through a sort of voting system with majority rule.

A spiritualist, whose cause is the easiest to "prove," simply says, "See, any of these reports proves that there is an afterlife." A liberal Christian claims, "Yes, and all twenty of my subjects said that they saw heaven." Then an orthodox Christian claims in rebuttal, "Ah, yes, but what you don't realize is that I have resuscitated thirty people who saw hell." But the death blow is apparently delivered to the orthodox Christian when the Hindu Vedantist comes along and claims,

"Not all of your beings-of-light were this Christ being; five of our international subjects reported Krishna, two saw Buddha, and we found any number of ascended masters. Besides, there are variant realms of death planes, not just heaven and hell." Even if the orthodox Christian drums up ten thousand cases that support his belief, just a handful of exceptions blows his watertight argument.

The Christians have rushed headlong into this maze, naively oblivious to the bottleneck farther along the way that will trap them. But I can now submit that there is an entire range of knowledge that has been almost totally omitted in previous attempts to untangle this mystery of "clinical death" reports. And with this, a wholly new pattern has emerged which clarifies the puzzle.

Several different approaches to understanding death are prevalent in the world today. In one tradition, mystics, gurus, and mediums claim the authority of firsthand experience. These related categories are covered in Section Two of this book, which is about psychics and mediums, as well as in Section Three, which is about death in the East.

Then there is the scientific approach, whereby men attempt to somehow rationally and experimentally understand life and death, as well as the philosophical approach, whereby men, through the intellect alone, try to reason out and philosophize the meanings of life, death, and existence. These two related categories are dealt with in Section Four, which is about death in the West.

Section Five, the final category, is about the biblical tradition, which provides for the possibility of the very God of the universe to speak to the hearts and minds of men (prophets) in order to reveal the truths of existence, life, death, and himself.

The categories mentioned above fit into three major traditions: the biblical tradition, the Western tradition, and the Eastern or ancient tradition.

The names are self-explanatory. Since the Eastern tradition can be traced back to the ancient mystery religions, it is sometimes referred to as "the ancient tradition." The modern phenomena of the psychics are in the ancient tradition, because they are not modern at all; their roots are ancient.

FOREWORD

Psychics appear in ancient Egypt, Chaldea, Persia, Babylon, Greece, and India. The psychics and mediums were the very oracles of Babylon and ancient Greece.

The psychics claim to have the most ancient and direct access to the secrets and realities behind the mystery of death. They have permeated many cultures, though Babylon was the most famous. Now they have gained a very prominent voice here in the West. Books by and about a number of famous psychics and mediums are best sellers. Societies are founded in their names, such as Edgar Cayce's Association for Research and Enlightenment (A.R.E.), Arthur Ford's Spiritual Frontiers Fellowship, The Theosophists, The Rosicrucians, and The Brotherhood of the Seven Rays. The Masons dabble in psychic sciences, and Jean Dixon, whose columns fill newspapers around the world, is a psychic.

Psychics have been included within the inner circles of numerous governments, from Franklin D. Roosevelt's presidency to Hitler's Third Reich. TV specials show psychics in action, such as Uri Geller bending a knife merely by staring at it, Peter Hurkos solving the Boston Strangler murders, or Ted Serios staring down the lens of a camera and mentally projecting an image on unexposed film. Almost all of these psychics claim to be in touch with beings "on the other side." Geller claims that he does not receive his powers from any hidden source within his mind, but directly through beings with whom he is in contact, who channel their powers through him.

Dr. Raymond Moody, a medical doctor who also has a doctorate in philosophy, mentions that many of his subjects who "returned from death" have become psychic. Indeed, the common pattern of his subjects fits most readily into the pattern of psychic experience and mediumistic contacts with the beyond. Perhaps this is why Dr. Elisabeth Kubler-Ross, a psychiatrist and an associate of Moody's, confessed her use of mediums as primary source material. She found that the mediums contacted the same sources that her subjects did.

In essence, psychics and mediums claim that they can pass into the spirit world, or the realm of the dead, with as much ease as a person can walk through a door to get to another room. They claim that this realm is really another dimension, invisible in form, which intersects our physical universe. They assert that the inner spirit within them has access to both the physical dimension of everyday life and the spiritual dimension of deceased people and other types of beings. For a psychic to pass through this door, he has to "enter the deep unconscious realm of his spirit," become oblivious to this world, and commune with the other world. This is called a trance. It is the link between both worlds. The body of knowledge that psychics and mediums have claimed to have amassed across the ages is either from their entering this realm "astrally" in a "spirit body" or through contact teachings from departed spirits or higher spiritual beings. A familiar term for these higher beings is "being of light."

I am a former psychic. As a child I had numerous experiences, such as clairvoyance, telepathy, out-of-the-body experiences, and sensitivity to "spirits." Perhaps the main door opened when I obtained a Ouija board when I was ten. But I am no longer a psychic. I am a Christian. Therefore, when I try to pinpoint what I think are crucially important facts, I do it from a position of legitimate authority. Perhaps we also can bring into honest question some of the abundant enthusiasm and optimism that Kubler-Ross projects on the public in her present proselytizing of the psychic viewpoint. I am being as honest in my reaction as she is in hers, though I have tried to keep my reaction out of the picture. However, I cannot interfere with the data, which comes from primary sources which are best sellers, or my personal experiences with the psychics of these best sellers.

As a direct approach to seeing if the psychic teachings agree with the Bible, as they claim to do, we are going to "open the case" in a courtroom fashion, occasionally pitting the psychic tradition's statements against the biblical tradition. Then, if there is true unity, it will become abundantly clear; if not, that, too, will clear the air.

SECTION ONE
THE ISSUE

ONE
SUDDEN DEATH

You're thundering down a highway to beat the miles of solid rush-hour traffic. Already dark at five o'clock, it's drizzling, misty, and the air seems heavy with oncoming winter. Pylons to the side, overpasses ahead, and a thousand headlights blur to form a dreary picture. Headlights charge out of passing side ramps. Suddenly there's a loud explosion. Peripherally faint voices seem to scramble about you; in the distance, sirens approach. Just enough of you is left to know that something unthinkable has happened, involving a semitrailer truck which jackknifed into the side of your car.

The next moment, with an incredibly airy feeling, you're floating near a ceiling and looking down upon an unsettling scene. Your body appears to be strapped to a table in a nest of tubes, wires, and gadgets. Frantically working while surrounding the body is a group of doctors, nurses, and medical technicians.

Your EEG is flat, there's no pulse, no respiration. Despite desperate efforts by the cardiac unit, they can't get your heart to beat. You may not have actually heard them, but you are aware that you have just been declared "clinically dead." In a moment, you will exit from the scene. What's in store for you may be the most bizarre thing you've ever experienced or thought of.

Like a ball bearing being jetted through an infinite shotgun, you're being hurled along some black tunnel. Time is not exactly the same; your journey may be taking months or minutes. Loneliness and fear are beginning to consume you. You're afraid that this could last forever. There's no reference point, nothing familiar, for you have become a complete pawn in the hands of something, perhaps a process, larger than life.

But now the fear of the unknown, which had consumed you at first, begins to vanish. A light appears at the end of the tunnel, and the awful loneliness, which you had thought might go on forever, is blotted out by some benign decree. Surrounding you, like fireflies, are distinct conscious entities or living personalities, and an inward eruption of joy tells you that on some deep, fundamental level, these are personalities that you recognize. They truly are your oldest friends, though they may even be millions of years old. What counterfeited itself as love and rapport on the earth is dwarfed by the sheer feeling of communion here. But at the end of the tunnel, in what seems the light of a thousand suns, their escort ends, and you are in the presence of something else—a superhuman being of pure radiance.

Its impact is different from the old biblical stereotypes that you had created in your mind. It is a great consciousness. In the fullest, most direct sense, it now probes into all that you are, penetrating your being with a complete and utter question regarding who you are, and the success or failure of your last life. A glib answer is out of the question.

Now, in what appears to be a blanket of total love, it extracts the full pictorial imagery of your life and hurls it onto some vast invisible screen. In awe, you watch your life speed by, while a probing, high-level dialogue critiques your past actions. The mistakes stand out, but they are bathed in forgiving love. Apparently you are to learn some lesson on a scale you never previously apprehended. Your life was just a tiny intermediate step in what may be a vast continuum of collective experience, which is leading you to some exalted destination, some state of being beyond your wildest dreams. It may well be that this being of light is the terminal point of the evolution of pure consciousness. It is a dazzling thought.

Just as the being of light responds to some goof of yours with a kindhearted, humorous aside, and a feeling grips you that you are cloaked in love and joy and never want to leave this condition or ever see the earth again, the same powerful force that brought you here sends you hurtling back through the long, dark tunnel. To your dismay, in only seconds you awake to a hand jamming an oxygen mask onto your face. You have been "brought back from the dead."

But wait a minute. A car horn blares at the side of your window, and you realize this has been pure reverie, a fantasy on the road as you navigate through rather dull and routine rush-hour traffic. It never really happened, but you hope it will. You anticipate it with more certainty than Walter Mitty's behind-the-wheel fantasies of becoming a ship's captain one minute or the President of the United States the next. The ideas, of course, are not yours. You have gotten them from the media's proclamation of the latest scientific breakthrough into the mystery of death. Now it's only a matter of waiting it out and trying a little harder before you, too, encounter your own being of light!

With little more than a brief shrug, you have accepted the newest, sleekest, most updated "scientific" model of the events of death. But here is the urgent question: Is it the absolute truth, so proven that we can gear our entire lives in terms of it? Is it really a fully accurate picture of death in the tradition of the purest scientific methodology, or is it only packaged as proven material, dazzling us with a format which we have learned to trust implicity? There has to be an answer if life truly has meaning, especially if the Author of existence has put a high premium on this subject.

We are about to cover an unusual range of categories in our probe. At times we will plunge into the annals of recorded thought, spanning the range from the yogis of the East and the philosophers and mystics of the West, to those who claimed to be truly God-inspired in the Middle East. Eternity may well be at stake after all.

TWO
THE NEW BREAKTHROUGH

The mystery of death gripped me even when I was a small child. It was something no one was free from, and it could spring unannounced upon almost anybody, carrying the force of a hurricane multiplied umpteenfold. I sensed that if anybody could figure out where it led, he would have a profound handle on ultimate truth. The invention of all time would be the discovery that could bring back the dead. One Sunday morning when I was nine years old, I remember pining wistfully over the news picture of a pretty girl who had died during an epileptic attack. Though I did not know her, I felt overwhelming loss. In a sense it was the ultimate indignity, but no amount of thought could penetrate the dense cloud of unknowing. The authorities of the adult world around me were at a loss for explanation.

Then when I was twelve I stood at a bookrack and discovered *The Case for Bridey Murphey*. I learned a new word: *reincarnation*. The book unfolded the amazing story of Bridey Murphey going from regressive hypnosis across the great divide to a previous life as a girl in Ireland. It was incredible. It occurred to me that if even one case could be substantiated, my view of life would be changed radically. It meant that I was old, for the age of our bodies was irrelevant to our spiritual age. If we reincarnated even once, who could limit the number of times it might happen? I felt a sense of relief.

Then, later, other things became linked with the Bridey Murphey scheme as I began to read a popular parapsychic journal, *Fate Magazine*. Maybe ghosts were spirits caught between incarnations.

When I was fifteen, another door was pried open. Ben, a friend of mine, had a tonsillectomy. After the operation at a hospital in Beirut, Lebanon, he was left with a most peculiar and vivid memory. He had left his body for a time. Shooting out in an exuberant rush of energy, he had soared up into a stratosphere of sublime hues as the pandemonium below vanished almost out of sight. The "cord" leading to his body would only let him go so high—to the edge of the earth's barrier. But there he met a spirit that said he had been killed in Korea. Just then, Ben was yanked back inside his body. For days we both jubilated over his experience.

Sporadically, over the next ten years, other pieces of the puzzle fell into place, finally forming a picture of death almost identical to what recent thanatologists like Dr. Raymond Moody have proclaimed. Edgar Cayce, a psychic in Virginia Beach, Virginia, had said a lot about it, and a few massive doses of LSD sealed it off for me, until I walked around in such a closed bottle of spiritual certainty that proof to the contrary would have barely dented my wall of beliefs. On the other hand, if a scientist had appeared with evidence backing up my beliefs, I would have seized it with joy. I was infatuated with my new sense of spiritual freedom.

What I did not realize was that my view of death fit into a tradition that was only one option among a handful of traditions; my view was molded from ideas that had filtered from the East, and its root in history went back to ancient India, Babylon, Chaldea, and Egypt. What I failed to consider was that another great tradition existed whose alternative, equally weighty, was not necessarily in accord with what I believed. What the world needed was a scientist to supply proof which would settle the debate between the great traditions, once and for all.

Dr. Moody and Dr. Elisabeth Kubler-Ross have made their debut, appearing to be those scientists for whom I might have hoped, and the world is eagerly devouring their discoveries, which seem so appropriate for our age. Their discoveries are "based on experiences," or at least internal experiences; and though they cannot be controlled by using the laboratory method, they appear to be phenomena, though they are not directly observable. Still, one wonders what is really new. Throughout history various persons have claimed to have had certain types of experiences as visionaries, mystics, people in the saucer cults, and so on. What needed to be settled was the issue of ultimate reality, not different categories of private experience. Either God was or was not. Then, if he did exist, what was his true nature? By this we would learn that some experiences were real, while others were more like hallucinations or mirages. What was needed was a reliable criterion. Science has seemed to be the answer, though it is a self-limiting field by definition.

How objective is the scientist? Moody, in the introduction to *Life After Life*, submits that his book, "written as it is by a human being, naturally reflects the background, opinions and prejudices of its author."[1] That is true; I knew Moody quite well in college and can vouch for our mutual interest in the more mystical interpretation of existence, for we both speculated about reincarnaton and related subjects. Our mutual friend, George Ritchie, in his own death experience, taught that reincarnation was a definite reality, and that what many of the Eastern mystics taught was a reality which fit into a more liberal picture of "Christ consciousness."

The gist of *Life After Life* is that beneath the neat scientific reporting is a distinct framework of reality which draws upon the testimony of fifty "clinical deaths" to yoke, by implication, the world religions by analogy. Moody maintains that there is a link, if you use a certain slant, between Hinduism, Buddhism, and Christianity in their teachings about death, and that after death the soul lives on (which apparently agrees with all religions), evolves (love and knowledge being the spiritual universals sought), and very possibly reincarnates. As Kubler-Ross would contend, we begin to see death and its workings in the universe as a laboratory for spiritual evolution. At the end of his book, Moody clearly states that his work does not constitute any sort of proof by scientific criteria. Rather, it all seems to be in a strange new category of its own, a modern enigma that touches science and religion, which perhaps has only been possible with the advent of sophisticated medical equipment that can "keep the dead from dying" or revive those thought dead.

The heart of Moody's discovery is the following model of what happens at death, an ideal composite of fifteen elements which have a high statistical occurrence among his subjects, though no case had all fifteen and only a few had twelve or more:

> A man is dying and, as he reaches the point of greatest physical distress, he hears himself pronounced dead by his doctor. He begins to hear an uncomfortable noise, a loud ringing or buzzing, and at the same time feels himself moving very rapidly through a long dark tunnel. After this, he suddenly finds himself outside his own physical body, but still in the immediate physical environment, and sees his own body from a distance, as though he is a spectator. He watches the resuscitation attempt from this unusual vantage point and is in a state of emotional upheaval.
>
> After a while, he collects himself and becomes more accustomed to his odd condition. He notices that he still has a "body," but one of a very different nature and with very different powers from the physical body he has left behind. Soon other things begin to happen. Others come to meet and to help him. He glimpses the spirits of relatives and friends who have already died, and a loving, warm spirit of a kind he has never encountered before—a being of light—appears before him. This being asks him a question, nonverbally, to make him evaluate his life and helps him along by showing him a panoramic, instantaneous playback of the major events of his life. At some point he finds himself approaching some sort of barrier or border, apparently representing the limit between earthly life and the next life. Yet, he finds that he must go back to the earth, that the time for his death has not yet come. At this point he resists, for by now he is taken up with his experiences in the afterlife and does not want to return. He is overwhelmed by intense feelings of joy, love, and peace. Despite his

attitude, though, he somehow reunites with his physical body and lives.[2]

Moody goes on to describe, in the course of his book, how the recovered subject goes out into a truth-rejecting world which forces him to conceal what he knows. As was true in past history, we learn that there will be a certain amount of witch hunting before the world becomes acclimated enough to the truth to accept it.

How are we to understand these baffling phenomena in a materialistic world which makes no provision for such things? The answer is given in Moody's chapter entitled "Parallels." This is where the syncretism of the world religions occurs, but it takes a certain slant to succeed. Part of the slant is a theological error. The Bible, according to Moody, "has relatively little to say about the events that transpire upon death, or about the precise nature of the after-death."[3] Then he cites several passages which in an oblique way appear to relate to his discoveries (out-of-body experiences and beings of light). In the mysticism of Plato and Emanuel Swedenborg, the parallel sticks; but when Moody mentions the secret teachings in *The Tibetan Book of the Dead*, the kernel of his discoveries is fully described and endorsed by no less than Eastern mystics scores of centuries before our modern age. That is a potent clue to who has the answer. Moody says, "The correspondence between the early stages of death which it [*The Tibetan Book of the Dead*] relates and those which have been recounted to me by those who have come near to death is nothing short of fantastic."[4] The Tibetan book, however, goes on to describe further phases of the death journey which Moody's subjects were unable to reach: realms of souls, planes of being, hell worlds, paradise planes, illuminated gods, and the secrets of transmigration. The thing to do, if this is the case, is to seek those Tibetans who have experienced the complete death journey. (This is what I did in 1969 when I went to India and studied under the yogis, as anyone who is serious about pursuing this subject would do.)

If *The Tibetan Book of the Dead* has been sitting quietly with all the secrets which we in the West have missed, this opens the doors to its brother and sister books of India, such as

The Upanishads, The Srimad Bhagavata, The Bhagavad Gita, The Puranas, Vedas, Sutras, and Ramayana. If that door opens, the writings of the yogis have to be fair game. One's authority must become the writings of Ramanah Maharishi, Yogananda, Meher Baba, Vivekananda, Sri Aurobindo, Ramakrishna, Patanjali, and Shankaracharya.

What does Shankaracharya teach, for instance? That the primary stage of learning comes when the aspirant dissociates his "self" from his physical body. "You are not your body." In fact, the body is to be mentally discarded (the path of Varaigya), for it is only transient and hence illusory. This is step one toward the mystical philosophy implied in Moody's documentation of consciousness as an entity apart from the body, where release is a "relief."

Step two toward mystical philosophy in Moody's findings is the possibility of reincarnation, which he leaves open. He suggests we read Ian Stevenson's *Twenty Cases Suggestive of Reincarnation*. (Dr. Stevenson, who was formerly on the faculty at the University of Virginia, where we were, was an associate of Dr. Ritchie.) Reincarnation is a mechanism of "soul evolution" in Hinduism and pantheism. It is through various bodies that the self reaches identity or becomes one with the godhead.

Step three toward Eastern religion in Moody's scheme is the "being of light." Time and again in the writings of the yogis, their deceased masters visit them in the form of a being of light. Other times, different gods visit them as forms of light (*Jyothir Murthi*, "god-form of light"). Sri Yukteshwar and Lahiri Mahasaya both visited Parmahamsa Yogananda from the astral plane as masters of light, and Ramakrishna saw his goddess, Kali, as a brilliant being of light. Kubler-Ross has a spirit guide too.

Step four in Moody's discoveries is the new (really *old*) view of good and evil. The Hindus view good and evil as illusions. Indeed, all pairs of opposites are unresolved illusions which can only be dissolved in the "oneness of the universe." If it is all one, good and evil are ultimately joined. The Hindus define "evil" ultimately as ignorance or any obstacle in the path of evolution. In case after case of astral encounter, the subject testifies that the being of light did not judge or condemn, but merely exuded great love and warmth, bringing the subject to a deeper knowledge of himself in which good and evil became subservient to his evolutionary needs. Evil comes to mean that the subject has not grown sufficiently or has not "loved" enough. Good and evil, therefore, are not distinctively antithetical and absolute qualities of which the Bible speaks. To get beyond the "primitive" idea of absolute good and evil is an evolutionary technique, basic to all forms of yoga and mystical thought. Interestingly, it is also promulgated by the Satanists (Aleister Crowley, Anton LaVey, Sybil Leek) and psychic mediums (Jane Roberts, Arthur Ford, etc.).

How does the being of light deal with the problem of evil? It is a being of liberal, "loving" permissiveness that counters our sins with "good vibrations." On the "other side," there is not so much punishment as there is cause-and-effect feedback for the higher good of the soul. Sin against others is minimized, often in jocular humor, which the being of light often engages in when reviewing the subject's life. Not even a whisper of a mention is made about sin against God (a root biblical concept).

When I picked up the Bridey Murphey book as a young boy, I did not realize that since history's beginning a distinct antithesis or warring has existed between two major traditions of thought and spirituality. Two alternatives of perspective (one perilous) were in the Garden of Eden. When Israel was chosen by God as a nation, there was the Chaldean-Babylonian religious system, which the God of the Jews opposed, forbidding his people to have any dealings with their religious "abominations." God told them of the differences which separated the living God of the Jews from the secret mysteries of the Babylonians. Israel and Babylon represent the perennial struggle between the direct, exoteric, universal, and absolute revelation of God sovereignly intervening in history, as opposed to the occult, esoteric, gnostic mysteries of a man-based mystical pursuit of self-evolution (even to the point of merging with God). Their views of death contrast as sharply as all their other areas of disagreement, as we shall see. Consider, for example, that the crowning lie of the adversary, through the serpent, was the proclamation to Eve, "Ye shall not surely die" (Gen. 3:4).

In Revelation, the last book of the Bible, is a prediction about a future worldwide reappearance of Babylon, with all its ancient mysteries, reigning as the religion of the world. Called "Mystery Babylon," it is ingenious, so clever in its metaphysical system of counterfeit spiritual truths that it seduces the entire world system, unifying it into a one-world religion. Unity under the banner of love and growth is its platform promise, desirable now at all costs; this seems good, so the world accepts it (Genesis 3:6 says that Eve found the fruit good and desirable). But Revelation says "Mystery Babylon" is really the ancient enemy of God and, like the Babylon of old, it will present death as an angel of light, a dear friend, a fragrant visitation, a bliss realm of the music of the spheres, in perfect accord with the present Eastern mystical view of death. Only one major view challenges it, and Revelation proclaims that view also, with awesome power. Our aim must be to examine carefully the real implications of each side.

THREE
FINDING
A DEFINITION
FOR DEATH

Before going to the "other side," let us find an acceptable definition of death that we all can agree on. When is someone really dead? What is a standard on which medicine, law, and common sense can agree?

We certainly would be doubtful about reports of someone who "died" every afternoon at three o'clock, who snored through the experience, and revealed his tales of the other side as he rubbed the sleep out of his eyes. We would suspect he had been dreaming.

Yet what are we to say about the new hard-to-define nether worlds which are the recent products of medical technology? Was the patient dead whose electroencephalogram (EEG) floated for two hours? Opinion is divided. "Clinical death" is a more chimerical gray region than one might think.

For the *Life After Life* study that Moody did, there were two general categories of subjects: those diagnosed as "clinically dead," and those who merely came close to death and reported their experiences. So the essence of Moody's report is among that minority of clinically dead out of the fifty subjects interviewed. We know that the latter group never died, but what about the first group?

For one thing, John Weldon, coauthor of *Is There Life After Death?*, discovered at the outset of his investigation that a current problem exists among the authorities of even agreeing on a definition. Weldon observes, "Death had been defined recently in the courts as, 'Not a continuing event . . . [but] an event that takes place at a precise time.' Medical journals have it as, 'A process and not a moment in time.'"[1]

Weldon goes on to observe, "Considering those who were certified dead by machine—were they really dead, and how dead? There are still some problems here. Physicians, lawyers, and laymen ultimately disagree as to the moment or process of death."[2] And even physicians can disagree among themselves.

Are clinical-death patients who later revive perhaps an index not of death, but rather of the inadequacies of machine diagnosis? A machine seems to say for a while that a man is dead, but later it indicates life in the patient after all. Would a far more sensitive machine have registered "life" and not "death"?

A major current definition of death is "the absence of brain wave activity." This is a definition wholly dependent upon machine diagnosis. Is it 100 percent reliable?

"The EEG machine is a complicated one, difficult to set up, especially in emergency situations. Even practiced professionals are predisposed to confusion and error in the face of impending death. Getting correct readings is difficult. Secondly, there have been cases where flat EEG tracings (indicating no brain wave activity whatever) were obtained in people who were later resuscitated. This situation tends to occur in cases involving very low body temperatures. . . . Flat EEG readings in these cases (heart surgery etc.) have gone on for 24 hours in patients who then completely recovered."[3]

Then, too, disagreement exists among medical doctors as to how long the EEG reading should be flat before the patient is finally declared clinically dead. In hopes of preventing anyone from being murdered, "the National Academy of Medicine of France chose the 48-hour flat EEG reading for certifying death in the case of transplant donors."[4]

It appears from examining the results of our machine-diagnosed clinical death that we really do have a hit-or-miss situation. A subject is declared clinically dead *before* he has been found to be alive again after all. Did he die?

It becomes apparent that the clinical-death definition of

death is inadequate, for it has loopholes. It is not good enough to satisfy the demands of science, because it contradicts the idea of an irreversible decision. (It got its definition in the past because people did not come back. Like the gravedigger holding the skull, we knew so-and-so was dead.) But, in the past, medical practitioners found a very high correlation between "respiratory cessation," "cardiac arrest," complete "loss of vital signs," and the patients staying that way and not coming back.

Is there any other criterion besides clinical death? Yes, and it excludes every single one of Moody's subjects, as Moody himself anticipates.[5]

The most acceptable criterion for genuine and complete death occurs when the categories of "cardiac arrest," "respiratory cessation," "flat EEG," and "complete loss of vital signs" are satisfied and this condition remains permanent through rigor mortis and physical decay. When the body begins to smell from decay, one can be assured that it is dead, especially if it has been ice-cold for days and has gone through rigor mortis.

The only historical records of recoveries from this form of death are in the New Testament. Lazarus was stone cold and decaying for four days before he was brought back to live out the appointed remainder of his life. Death, apart from some really astounding miracle such as the case of Lazarus, is irreversible; that has to be the definition. If you protest this, then give us the death experience of a subject who has been dead four days and in decay, and we will be much more likely to be persuaded by the report.

But we are still left with a question. If Moody's subjects were never really dead, how do we explain their common pattern of experience? What is the origin or source of these experiences? As in any sound investigation, we will be pressed to look for other common patterns or precedents in history and ask, When, where, and in what context have the same experiences occurred before? Thanatologist Kubler-Ross strays from "science" occasionally and breathes a clue as to where to look; it is in the category of psychic mediums, psychics, yogis, and Eastern masters. "From my interviews with the dying and with MEDIUMS, I would describe the other world as similar to ours."[6] As we shall find out, her dealings in the "other traditions," the psychic occult, have been more than superficial. She herself has a spirit guide with whom she has been in contact for years. What we need to discover is whether there is a common ground linking yoga, Eastern beliefs, psychic teachings, and mediumistic contacts, especially if they converge so closely in their reports and proclamations about the nature of death. It may well turn out that all these groups stem from a common source; indeed, they could well be the new Babylonians.

Moody's clinically dead may be in a state that is far closer to a mediumistic trance or a yogic *samadhi* than real death. In *The Tibetan Book of the Dead*, a majority of the predeath reports on death came from yogis who had learned to enter a type of suspended animation. This still happens today. In October 1977, when I was in Delhi, a day-by-day, front-page news sensation concerned a yogi who was buried underground. He had managed to stop his heart for long periods, reduced his pulse rate to nil, lower his body temperature, and maintain a flat EEG. His gamble was that he could remain that way for ten days. The paper reported that when he had done the same thing in the 1960s, he was able to maintain the state for five days.[7] As we shall see later, yogis have traditionally sought this odd nether-world state; but because they came back and never showed the signs of absolute death, we know they never really died. Nor do they claim to have died.

If we were to try to figure out the mystery of existence, of life and death, we would have a limited number of options, which have been available for some time:

A. We could ingest a psychedelic such as LSD and allow the experience to tell us the hidden secrets of life.
B. We could find mystics, gurus, and yogis whose own experiences claim to solve our quest for ultimate truth.
C. We could seek our own mystical revelation, some inner consciousness-expansion.
D. We could attempt to use the instruments of science to somehow seek out the invisible parameters of life.
E. We could attempt, as did Immanuel Kant, to

apprehend the truth by sheer human reason. We would puzzle things out by using the logical and philosophical methods available, though we would probably end up like the rationalist philosophers limited to strictly observable phenomena which not even they, in the end, trusted.
F. Finally, we could be left with one main option. If the order and complexity of the universe somehow testified of an Author, Creator, or God . . . it might cross our minds that he himself might well reach down (if life does have a purpose), and shortcut what might be a fruitless search by telling, directly, certain absolute truths of life and existence to a whole lineage of people. This is known as divine revelation; history, archeology, and good honest observation show that this possibility is by no means foreclosed. It makes a tremendous amount of sense when you think about it.

Actually, these six subcategories (apart from the nihilist, existentialist view, which believes everything is an accident), fall in either of the two major religious traditions: (1) the occult, Babylonian, Eastern, pantheistic-monistic tradition, with its preceptors ranging from mediums, psychics, yogis, avatars, and so on; or (2) the biblical tradition, with its prophets, saints, apostles, and one Christ.

Almost every book today which tackles the problem of the meaning of life tries to yoke the biblical and occult traditions and say that they both reveal the same truth and that both point to the same God. Since the life-after-death issue will inevitably lead us into one of these camps, we must examine whether they are compatible. Our conclusions about the two traditions will determine our attitudes toward death and will affect our behavior in life, so it is here we must begin.

SECTION TWO

EXPERIENCES OF THE BEYOND— PSYCHICS, MEDIUMS, AND THE OCCULT

FOUR
THE PSYCHIC DEATH EXPERIENCE

Our battle is to bring down every deceptive fantasy and every imposing defence that men erect against the true knowledge of God (2 Cor. 10:5, 6, Phillips).

On many freezing winter nights in 1968, I motorcycled down the dark wooded lanes weaving from Charlottesville, Virginia, to the spectral ranch house of Robert Monroe, author of *Journeys out of the Body*, poised on its many acres and beaming multicolored lights like an airport control tower. We often met several times a week. Monroe was famous across America among connoisseurs of the underground new-consciousness movement as a legitimate astral projector (one able to leave the physical body). Charles Tart and an array of notable parapsychologists had repeatedly run a whole gamut of double-blind tests on Monroe, invariably baffled each time by his unaccounted for powers.

Monroe and I originally met at a meeting of the Universal Youth Corps, which was founded by Dr. George Ritchie, a mystic and medical doctor to whom Dr. Moody dedicated his best seller, *Life After Life*, and who recently published the full account of his own death experience in *Return from Tomorrow*, Chosen Books, 1978. But by 1968 Ritchie had disbanded that group (though he remained in personal contact with some of us) because of some higher revelation.

Monroe, a board member of the Universal Youth Corps, was among the guest speakers to address the corps, along with Bryant Reeves, author of *Flying Saucer Pilgrimage* and a board member of Edgar Cayce's Association for Research and Enlightenment (A.R.E.). Monroe shared the enigmas of his many out-of-the-body travels. These enigmas later bound Monroe and me together in our quests following the dissolution of Ritchie's youth corps.

Monroe and I tried to make sense out of the whole phenomenon of astral travel, catalyzing one another in the process. He was approaching the subject in terms of the "higher teachings" he had received while out of the body in his encounters with "higher beings, astral masters, and beings of light," combined with his diversified readings in yoga, Eastern thought, and scientific theory. I was approaching his bizarre exploits and spirit encounters (plus a few of my own) from the viewpoint of nondualist Indian philosophy, through the perspective of my own 1966 mystical LSD experience—at which time I had experienced total unity of the universe—combined with a sort of mystical Christianity (along the lines of Ritchie, Cayce, Carl Jung, Paul Tillich, and Teilhard de Chardin). But, to Monroe, perhaps my most important credential was that apparently I, too, had been able to leave my physical body. It had started when I was an eleven-year-old child battling the mumps in London. Half asleep in bed, I would become paralyzed, hear the sound of jets, and apparently go ripping through the roof to hover above our house. Occasionally the same thing happened during my teens, and it was starting again in college. Monroe's out-of-the-body symptoms matched mine point for point.

During this era, I unwittingly found myself working with Monroe on the tape prototypes that eventually would become the M-5000 program, a complex, multichannel recorded tape which would be used across the country to induce astral experiences in the uninitiated. Cables and sound equipment trailed through the house from central command, an isolated geodesic chamber of pyramidal glass which rippled with colored lights, while pulse generators whirred and hummed to the syncopated beats of an organ. Monroe had been a child prodigy, spending much of his life dabbling with inventions

THE PSYCHIC DEATH EXPERIENCE

(much of his experience coming from his New York era as vice-president of Mutual Broadcasting).

But what was most momentous was that we were on the pioneering frontier of occult technology; indeed, it was from the "higher sources" that Monroe received the technological formulations of his endeavor (Monroe had a long list of technological breakthroughs that had been inspired by spirit contacts, the invention of the Xerox machine being a prime example). We were not closing the gap to enter the spiritual dimensions by blindly putting together the machinery. The powers on the other side had bridged the gap, with Monroe as medium, and were telling him exactly how to put things together. It is important that this be understood.

To be sure, our exploits had an air of intrigue. Imagine transforming America into a spiritual technology, with at least half the population astral traveling one day! According to Monroe, Ritchie, Cayce, and others, such large-scale mass spirituality has not been seen since the "days of Atlantis" (an advanced mythical civilization, once supposedly in the Atlantic, which is most highly spoken of in psychic circles).

But I still had problems with Monroe's "contact teachings" because they did not coincide with what I then considered the highest truth of all: the ultimate oneness of all things, which is the heart of Indian philosophy. To me, his "contact teachings" from astral classes were little more than fragmented interpretations of reality taught by demigods, beings of light, or spirits, which certainly were higher up than most humans, but still fell short of "the Absolute." As the Hindus would say, even that was a part of *maya* ("the illusory bondage of the ephemeral universe of appearances"). I tried to convince Monroe that the highest truth was the concept of the "static eternal" taught by Ramakrishna and the Indian mystics, for I was sure these sages had gone deeper than the meanderings of intermediate demigods. This fact alone eventually caused a split between Monroe and me. I went on to India, while he pursued his quest for the M-5000 and beyond.

Yet an aspect of some of our encounters threatened both our notions of a peril-free universe void of absolute evil (the "cosmic playground" approach). Some of these spirit encounters had a brutal, almost demonic, concreteness. This cut away at the stereotype I was forming of an almost symphonically gentle and peace-pervading cosmos whose evil was so wispy and illusory that apparent evil was little other than beneficent playacting.

One Saturday morning in the spring, Monroe looked quite shaken as he rubbed his bleary eyes over a cup of coffee at our usual meeting place, the kitchen table. I had spent a fitful night alone in a far-wing bedroom, with earphones on while lying flat on my back in an attempt to enter what I called "the buzz region." Apparently Monroe had been assaulted by something at about three in the morning, and the encounter continued until dawn.

"I felt about as significant as an ant compared to these two beings," Monroe started off. He said he had perceived clairvoyantly two massive beings of light, brighter than stars and of vast power, drifting deep in the heavens like two meteors. Then they had stopped their drift and honed in on him, beginning a terrible drilling down upon him like huge, sparking hornets. They descended with great speed while Monroe remained in the paralyzed "buzz state." Reaching his room, they impersonally did speed reading of the hidden records of his mind, flashing through his mind like flipping through a card file. After ten minutes they evidently had gotten what they wanted—or, as he suggested later, implanted what they wanted—and then they pulled away, much like a huge hypodermic being pulled out of a patient. This experience brought up the question of victimization and cosmic bullying, but we preferred to theorize more in the direction that the incident was an act of charity, that the two beings probably had left a subtle implant which would germinate years later—perhaps as a clue to spiritual technology.

In a guarded manner, Monroe said that these two beings might have some connection with unidentified flying objects. He believed UFOs were not necessarily machines, but celestial beings, almost angels of a sort. Now and then, late at night, Monroe would drive on higher impulse to the area of Browns Mountain. Odd phenomena would occur, but he would not say much about it. Browns Mountain, in the

Virginia Blue Ridge Mountains, was a notorious location for unusual occurrences, especially UFOs.

One common bond between Monroe and Ritchie was the UFO question and its role in what they saw as the coming changes on earth. (The answer for this whole problem is intelligently and convincingly set forth in the only manner possible that is consistent with biblical revelation in John Weldon's book, *UFOs: What on Earth Is Happening?* His thesis is that these strange phenomena, which have been documented so many times, are really spiritual phenomena, both deceptive and Satanic in nature.)

In the winter of 1972, a week after I returned from two years in India, I was invited by Ritchie to speak at a retreat in Massanetta Springs, Virginia, and again join his Universal Youth Corps. Ritchie disclosed something to an audience of two hundred people that finalized the tie between his mission and Monroe's. (It was also something that soon created a barrier between Ritchie and myself, for by then I was a former mystic and had become an evangelical Christian.) Ritchie announced that in 1958, at a corps retreat at the Peaks of Otter, he had an experience one night that revealed his true mission on the earth. A voice (whom he called "God") told him to leave his tent and go out on the mountain. It then instructed him to observe the firmament of brilliant lights above, which he did. Next it told Ritchie that these lights were massive "mother ships, UFOs of five miles in diameter, numbering sixty thousand," and poised waiting for the celestial command to come swooping down to pick up the remnant of true believers on the earth before our planet plunged into darkness and catastrophe. Ritchie was informed that he was the new Noah of this age and that the vehicles used would be flying saucers. Like Abraham, Ritchie was promised that many would be in his fold.

My reaction, of course, was amazement. Biblical exegesis clearly showed that God did not need to rely on the technology of spaceships to bring about his will. Indeed, what I was hearing was a demonization of biblical apocalyptic language, which ultimately denied Christ's second advent as well as God's sovereign power over history. Ritchie's vision fit perfectly into another arena that the Bible has predicted:

counterfeit teachings of truth, which would increasingly deluge the world through false prophets and false Christs (Matt. 24:24).

Monroe and Ritchie could both boast of experience, but what was the primary source of their individual inspirations? A being of light! Ritchie is the unspoken superstar of Moody's book. Ritchie's death experience, the grandest of all, occurred in Barkeley, Texas, in the mid 1940s. He says he encountered a "being of light brighter than ten billion arc welders," which proceeded to take him on a tour of the universe via different death planes and astral levels. Behind it all is the cosmology of reincarnation and of man perfecting himself to become God, a being of light. Karma emerges, along with all the other pantheistic notions. Christ, Ritchie says, is a being of light. But that is not what the Bible says of the ascended Son of God, who is above "every name that is named" (Eph. 1:21).

There is one Christ, but many beings of light. Let us look into this network of beings and discern the intentions behind their variant theologies. One predominant theme emerges: they have an obsessive preoccupation with Christ. Somehow they must deal with him before they can go on. Appearing to be loyal to biblical tradition, they obscure the simple heart of the gospel message. Naturally, they speak through people; their ideas come through human channels, mediums.

Invariably, they distort Christ so that he becomes a different Christ. As Paul the apostle warned in Galatians 1:6-9 (Phillips),

> I am amazed that you have so quickly transferred your allegiance from Him Who called you in the grace of Christ to another "gospel"! Not, of course, that it is or ever could be another gospel, but there are obviously men who are upsetting your faith with a travesty of the Gospel of Christ. Yet I say that if I, or an angel from heaven, were to preach to you any other gospel than the one you have heard, may he be damned!

It becomes apparent that "somebody" does not want biblical teaching to be accepted as it is without being filtered through another system, which is a most elaborate and costly strategy. As the old missionary saying goes, "Satan will use ninety-nine parts of the truth just to float one single lie." Yet most of these "Christs " that we shall examine barely contain one-tenth of the truth.

We already have seen that the beings of light reviewed by Moody disavow biblical judgment. Christ becomes a being of light, reincarnation is offered as a viable option, and God is almost avoided entirely. Is there a common pattern among the most famous mediums? What do the beings of light say through them?

Let us examine the maze a little more closely. First, there is Edgar Cayce, the clear-eyed, bespeckled Kentuckian who looked as honest as the day is long. A veritable Bible-Belt medium, he originally won my heart by his heartening, almost sentimental, allegiances to Christ, and the reverential tones in which he couched his deviant teaching. This man of such plain and humble demeanor seemed to be far from any calculating card shark. Yet if we look in Proverbs, we find that there is more to judge than honest looks. A man can appear good and yet deceive. Second Corinthians 11:15 says Satan's ministers are "as the ministers of righteousness."

Cayce helped me go to India. The "Christ" he was weaving fit perfectly into the philosophies of the East. This was a major bridge for me. The dialogue of his trance readings would go from an impersonal "we" of the so-called cosmic mind ("Akashic records") to a pseudo King James Bible talk of "ye" and "thee." What emerged from his filtering system was a most complex schema. Boiled down, it amounted to this: Christ was the perfect yogi, *avatar*, ("incarnation"), and God-man, who had reincarnated on the earth a number of times in setting up his messianic mission, perfecting himself with each life. Melchizedek was but one embodiment in Christ's genealogy of past lives. In that sense he becomes a model for all men to follow in order to attain what is now called "Christ-consciousness," a level of cosmic awareness at the pinnacle of soul evolution.

Along with rebirth comes the inevitable law of karma. Sin disappears and the biblical God vanishes into something that is more like Brahman. As Cayce gave people "life readings" concerning their past lives, they were told they were ex-high priests from Atlantis, ex-wizards and warlocks, psychic healers, and occasionally a former disciple of Christ, doubtlessly returned to touch up here and there the blemishes of the past.

One biographer compiled a book just about Cayce's teachings on Christ by sifting through thousands of "life readings" filed at the A.R.E. at Virginia Beach. What emerges, of course, is an emphasis on the hidden years of Christ's life, about which the Bible is silent. With an elaborate discourse on astrological forces, we see the young "perfect Master" headed to Egypt to study at the temples of wisdom and beauty, where he learns certain psychic arts. Then he goes on to India and Tibet to learn levitation and transmutation from certain Tibetan masters; while in India, he learns healing, weather control, telepathy, and ultimately reaches atonement ("at-one-ment") with the divine overmind. From there he returns to the Holy Land as the fully promised Messiah.

Yet the apostles left out all this information. The Bible does not mention so much as a hint of it, and none of the historians of antiquity even had the slightest notion of any of this.

Practically all of the psychics, mediums, and mystics portray this brand of cosmic Christ. Levi Dowling fares no better. His book, *The Aquarian Gospel of Jesus the Christ*, was written in the later nineteenth century, while this Midwestern psychic and medical practitioner traveled from town to town in a covered wagon. This particular gospel, currently most popular and fashionable, was written through the medium from midnight to three in the morning as he gave his body over to a "higher force" to write through him. Its purpose? It completes what the apostles left out, updated for our present "Aquarian age," which is interesting considering the Bible's stand against the Babylonian occult science of astrology. Dowling, like the other mediums, started out early by a deliberate rejection of the Christian message.

Thomas Sugrue, the major biographer of Edgar Cayce in *There Is a River*, makes an observation that fits both Cayce and Dowling: "The system of metaphysical thought which emerges from the readings of Edgar Cayce is a Christianized version of the mystery religions of ancient Egypt, Chaldea, Persia, India, and Greece. It fits the figure of Christ into the tradition of one God for all people, and places Him in His proper place . . . He is the capstone of the pyramid."[1] This is far removed from the true biblical Christ, who is the chief cornerstone of the living Church.

Dowling portrays the "young Master" as a sort of Siddhartha, passing tortuous tests, transcending the limited ego, and going on sojourns through India, Tibet, Persia, Assyria, Greece, and Egypt.

To establish this point clearly, we will examine a number of statements from this higher gospel, the so-called Aquarian gospel. Of course, we see an entirely different story, teaching, and personality than what appears in the New Testament. Both cannot be right.

> And Jesus was accepted as a pupil in the temple Jagannath: and here learned the Vedas and Manic laws (21:19).
>
> Benares of the Ganges was a city rich in culture and learning; here the two rabbonis tarried many days. And Jesus sought to learn the Hindu art of healing, and became the pupil of Udraka, the greatest of Hindu healers. Udraka taught the uses of the waters, plants, and earths; of heat and cold; sunshine and shade; of light and dark (23:2-4). [This is herbalist arts.]
>
> [Jesus teaches at the house of Udraka.] And Jesus said to them, With much delight I speak to you concerning life—the brotherhood of life. The universal God is one, yet he is more than one; all things are God; all things are One (28:3, 4). [This is pantheism, monism.]
>
> [Jesus hears of the grief of his mother over the death of Joseph, his "father." He assures her that Joseph's round of karma is completed.] Why should you weep? Tears cannot conquer grief. There is no power in grief to mend a broken heart. The Plane of grief is idleness; the busy soul can never grieve; it has no time for grief (30:11, 12). [This is a contradiction to his tears and indignation of spirit at the tomb of Lazarus.]
>
> [Jesus attends a feast in Persepolis and speaks to the people, reviewing the magician philosophy.] A feast in honor of the magician God was being held, and many men were gathered in Persepolis. And on the great day of

THE OTHER SIDE OF DEATH

the feast the ruling magician master said, Within these sacred walls is liberty; whoever wills to speak may speak. And Jesus standing in the midst of the people, said, My brothers, sisters, children of our Father-God; most blessed are you among the sons of men today, because you have just conceptions of the Holy One and man. Your purity in worship and in life is pleasing unto God; and to your master Zarathustra, praise is due. [He later explains to the magicians that their human will must merge into divine will.] (39:1-5). [This is occultic and synchretistic.]

[Jesus runs into the Oracle at Delphi.] Apollo said to Jesus, Sir, if you would see the Delphic Oracle, and hear it speak, you may accompany me. . . . And when Apollo stood before the Oracle it spoke and said: Apollo, sage of Greece, the bell strikes twelve; the midnight of the ages has come. . . . The Delphic age has been an age of glory and renown; the gods have spoken to the sons of men through oracles of wood, and gold, and precious stone. . . . The gods will speak to man by man. The living oracle now stands within these sacred groves; the Logos from on High has come (45:3-10). [Idolatry is justified; Christ becomes the oracle through which the gods are to speak.]

[In Heliopolis of Egypt, Jesus goes through the seven tests of the mystical brotherhood. Test number six is in the Chamber of the Dead.] The senior course of study now was opened up and Jesus entered and became a pupil of the Heirophant. He learned the secrets of the mystic lore of Egypt land; the mysteries of life and death and of the worlds beyond the circle of the sun. When he had finished all the studies of the senior course, he went into the Chamber of the Dead, that he might learn the ancient methods of preserving from decay the bodies of the Dead; and here he wrought. And the carriers brought the body of a widow's only son to be embalmed; the weeping mother followed close; her grief was great. And Jesus said, Good Woman, dry your tears; you follow an empty house; your son is in it not. You weep because your son is dead. Death is a cruel word; your son can never die (54:1-7). [This contradicts the Genesis curse and advocates astrology; Christ raised the dead, not embalmed them; it advocates the Egyptian mysteries, etc.]

To reiterate, in Dowling's book and Cayce's teachings is a "Christos" of the mystery religions and mystical orders; it is an Antichrist.

Arthur Ford, a Canadian billed constantly as "the greatest medium of the century," was the man who "turned on" Bishop James Pike. His Christ fits quite handily into the mold dictated by the so-called Spiritualist Church. Ford, who boasted, "I've slept for the best people," did a noteworthy job on Bishop Pike in adding to the delusion of the already apostate bishop.[2]

Indeed, what really launched spiritualism in America recently was the Bishop Pike incident. Pike once told theologian Francis Schaeffer that all he was left with after coming out of a liberal seminary was "a hand full of stones." After meeting Ford, however, he lost not only that, but more: his life. Proudly jettisoning plain biblical teaching, he was ripe for a "higher" breakthrough. It came in the form of a spirit masquerading as Jim, his dead son. His own crippled faith could not deal with Jim's death, so he turned to his son for the answer. Pike invited the public to watch a televised séance of himself and Ford. This potent propaganda presented the perfect opportunity for the spirits to teach the public about higher truth.

The so-called spirit of Jim originally started the contact by extensive poltergeist phenomena in the bishop's apartment—heat changes, levitating objects, disappearing objects, and, at one point, chopping off the bangs of a woman visitor, Maren Bergrud. Pike went to Ena Twigg, an English medium, and found out that the spirit was "Jim." Jim told the bishop, "Since I've been here, I haven't heard anything about Jesus." Some months later at another séance, Jim added, "This was religion without somebody forcing God and Jesus down my throat. . . . I haven't met [Jesus]. They talk about him—a mystic, a seer, yes, a seer. Oh, but Dad, they don't talk about him as a savior. As an example, you see? . . . Don't you ever believe that God can be personalized. He is the Central Force and you give your quota toward it. Do you agree with me, Dad?"[3] The bishop responded like a good dad should and jumped in with both feet, carrying a few million bystanders with him.

Ford played the largest role in unhinging Pike's theology and setting him up for the kill, ultimately directing the bishop and his new wife out to the Judean Desert. There they became stranded and the bishop wandered off into heat-filled mirages to die, while his young wife went off looking for help. Since then, the Ouija boards have been clacking away, heedless of biblical injunctions, to pick up the latest gleanings of higher truth from the now-departed bishop.

Now another pattern appears. Those mediums who did not start out by directly dabbling in the occult got their first boost by some kind of trauma. Allen Spraggett calls this a well-attested fact in his book, *Arthur Ford: The Man Who Talked with the Dead*. He adds, "Edgar Cayce, as a child, was knocked unconscious by a baseball and thereafter gave evidence of his remarkable powers. The contemporary Dutch-born clairvoyant, Peter Hurkos, fell off a ladder when he was twenty—lobotomizing himself—and woke up a mind reader."[4] Similar examples are cited by Spraggett regarding Ronald Ewin, D. D. Home, Clement Stone, and Arthur Ford.

Almost all of these mediums were exposed directly to Eastern mysticism—Cayce through a theosophist in Chicago, and Arthur Ford by delving into theosophy. Then in 1920 Ford met Yogananda, joined one of his yoga classes, started meditating, and "maintained years later" that it was "Yogananda who taught him how to induce a yogic trance, and, equally important, how to manipulate that altered state of consciousness for mediumistic purposes."[5] That is how Ford learned astral projection.

Therefore, it is not surprising that Ford, like the rest, also pushed the concepts of reincarnation, karma, and an impersonal pantheistic God.[6]

Spraggett, his biographer, sums it up: "For Arthur Ford, then, as for many spiritualists, Jesus Christ was a mirror of God; but he was not a quasi-divine savior whose death on the cross redeems man from sin."

"Spiritualists," Ford is quoted as saying in a 1930 sermon,

"can't depend on Christ. We must stand on our own feet. The spiritualist is the supreme individualist. We will eradicate our own sins, even though it takes a whole eternity in which to work them out!"

"Spiritualism," Spraggett observes, "like Buddhism, declares that man is his own savior, that the only salvation is self-salvation, that being saved by proxy is as impossible as learning by proxy, for, in both Buddhism and spiritualism, the key to salvation is right knowledge."

Ford's biographer then shares a most apropos declaration: "When we come to consider the distinctive teachings of Spiritualism, namely, its view of the afterlife and of communication between this world and the next, we find that it diverges even more markedly from traditional Christian thought."[7]

In line with most spiritualists, Kubler-Ross shared her own impressions of the afterlife when she said, "From my interviews with the dying and with mediums, I would describe the other world as looking similar to ours, except for the colors, which are very vibrant."[8]

Last but not least in the lives of mediums are their manner of life and the ends they come to. By the standard of Christ's teaching that you should know a man by his fruit (in the fullest sense of character and actions), mediums bear a rather wrinkled and sour fruit.

Ford was a miserable example of his own proud declaration, "We must stand on our own feet." Spraggett takes us through Ford's tortured personal life, his dope addiction, and then years of bouts with alcoholism, putting on a front before the public while pulling off mediumistic contacts, and then going back to long binges on the bottle. The famous medium died a wreck. His last words were, "God help me."[9]

The founders of modern spiritualism, Margaret and Kate Fox, who established spirit contact on March 21, 1848, and rose to prominence, also became alcoholics. They said the spirits had promised them protection, but it never came. "Craving for alcohol, they lost all sense of moral responsibility. Margaret, in the presence of her sister Kate at an anti-spiritualist meeting in 1888 declared, 'I am here tonight, as one of the founders of Spiritualism, to denounce it as absolute falsehood . . . the most wicked blasphemy the world has ever known.' "[10] As they died, both mediums cursed God.

Spraggett documents a long list of mediums who lived lives of turmoil and pain. "Besides alcoholism and drug addiction, sexual excesses or aberrations seem to be common among mediums. . . . Mediumship takes a toll in human suffering. Henry Slade, the famed nineteenth-century slate-writing medium, died penniless and alcoholic in a Michigan sanatorium. Stainton Moses, a scholarly medium who was an Anglican priest, disintegrated into abject alcoholism. Veiled eroticism lurked in the séance room of Eusapio Palladino. . . . Many male mediums have been homosexual, or ambisexual. Some psychical researchers go so far as to suggest that a certain sexual ambiguity is a part of the mediumistic temperament."[11]

I personally heard from a number of sources closely connected with the A.R.E. that, during his last two weeks of life, Edgar Cayce was in abject fear that his source of revelation was not the "Akashic Mind" but, instead, some kind of baleful spirit power. Medium Cayce died a Christless death without peace.

But one other witness, an exception, remains to be reviewed in our case. As a medium in London, he had contacted numerous spirits and beings of light, yet escaped the disastrous fate which befalls most mediums. How was Raphael Gasson spared? He became convinced that the source of his contacts was not the spirits of the departed, or higher beings of light, but, in fact, what he called "impersonating demons."

Gasson turned his life over to Jesus Christ, coming as a penitent sinner, without hope apart from Christ, and asking Christ to be his Lord and Savior. He suddenly realized that by the astoundingly holy standards of the living God, any effort on his part alone was futile. In contrast to Ford's proud declaration, Gasson *did* cry out for help, the sanest thing he could ever do. He was saved. Gasson claims that he was freed for the first time in his life, knew that he had a genuine reason for hope, and suddenly started changing as a person. In his book *The Challenging Counterfeit*, Gasson gives an inside look into the secrets of mediumship.

THE PSYCHIC DEATH EXPERIENCE

For one thing, he reveals that the seven principles of the Spiritualists National Union, founded in 1891, almost matched Moody's conclusions perfectly. Keep in mind that the major goal of spiritualism is to prove life after death precisely in the manner Moody has. The principles are: "1. The Fatherhood of God. 2. The Brotherhood of Man. 3. The communion of saints and the ministry of angels. 4. Human survival after physical death. 5. Personal responsibility to answer for one's own sins. 6. Compensation or retribution for good or evil deeds. 7. Eternal progress of every soul."[12]

The most amazing thing to me about Gasson's book is the last third, where he delves into the intricate dynamics of mediumship, matching much of what I had gleaned after years of studying and practicing yoga in India. Gasson discusses astral projection, vacating the mind, vacating the body, blanking out of consciousness, how the other personality takes over, and the eventual acquisition of the powers of telepathy, clairvoyance, materialization of spirit presences (in the manner of the visitation Kubler-Ross spoke of), levitation, healing, the seeing of auras, the apports of physical objects, supernatural knowing, and so on.

Gasson, like all the other mediums, believed in reincarnation. The soul, they say, evolves after so many countless lifetimes. Spiritualists use the concept of reincarnation to explain away misfortune in life. For example, the spiritualistic explanation of a stillborn infant is "a spirit who has evolved over and over again and all that is needed to attain perfection was just one more very short period in a physical body after which it becomes a spirit of the highest evolution straight away. This belief extends to animals and insects who are gradually evolving until they become human beings, and so on."[13] In India today, one commonly hears similar explanations. A child bitten by a snake is just working off karma ("the total record of his past: good vs. bad deeds"), and his next body will be much higher up. If an Indian infant dies, it is often explained as a very high sage or yogi coming just to work off a smidgeon of remaining bad karma. Then the yogi will reach "one with the absolute." (We begin to see that in more places than one the psychics, mediums, and spiritists are far closer in their beliefs to Hinduism than to biblical

Christianity.) But what exactly is a "spirit of the highest evolution possible" to which Gasson refers?

Gasson reveals something that is crucial to our understanding of this whole matter: "Having attained the highest evolution in the spirit world, one becomes A BALL OF LIGHT."[14] Where have we seen this before? The highest stage of spiritual evolution is the "ball of light" or, as other spiritualist camps refer to it, "a being of light." Here is a vital clue to understanding the significance of Moody's beings of light.

In many of the original reports, Moody's subjects referred to the being of light as a "ball of light." They testified that the reason for life, as they had learned in the spirit world, was for the soul's growth or evolution. It only takes a second to make the connection: the ultimate of spiritual growth is a state of existence whereby one becomes a being of light, which is a major tenet of spiritualism. The view of afterlife in Moody's best seller, *Life After Life*, is in full accord with the teachings of mediums, psychics, and spiritualists. This doctrine, formally propounded by a worldwide organization known as the Spiritualists or the Spiritualist Church, is aligned with another view known as "spiritism." Both doctrines are antithetical to biblical doctrines, as we shall see.

What can be known about the actual spirit world? Where do the dead go? After abundant research, it becomes clear that the picture changes from medium to medium. Kubler-Ross says tamely that the spirit world is like ours, only the colors are brighter. Pike's son, Jim, says it is not as good as he hoped, that it is sort of murky, but that he hopes to figure it out more one day. Psychics and mediums like Cayce, Ritchie, and Ford speak of varying levels of death planes; their views are the closest to the accounts in *The Tibetan Book of the Dead*. Ritchie's report of his "Barkeley, Texas, experience" goes from hell worlds of imprisoned spirits (presumably killers and all brands of scum) to the dismal realms of "earth-bound souls," where the spirits of departed alcoholics try to jump into the bodies of living alcoholics. We then see mediocre spirit planes, much like our world, on up to the plane which Ritchie describes as "a city of light," where there are "beings of light." Long before Moody wrote *Life After Life*, he heard

Ritchie give his account of the city of light and the beings of light. Ritchie says, and Moody intimates, that the ultimate destiny of the highest soul is to become a being of light and to live in the city of light. Many beings of light exist, including Christ, Buddha, and myriad others in their ranks.

But our search into the world of mediums and psychics does not end here. We must look even further to do justice to our inquiry. We need to see more clearly whether there is blatant evidence to help us determine whether the forces surging through the mediums are neutral, good, or evil. We need to ask the mediums, "How do you know you can trust a voice of something you have never seen? And if you tell me you know it is good, why should I trust you?" Now let us look at a few specific case studies.

FIVE
BEINGS OF LIGHT OR FALSE ANGELS OF LIGHT?

For Satan himself masquerades as an angel of light. So it is nothing extraordinary if his servants masquerade as servants of righteousness [Some of these servants, like Satan himself, are not enfleshed humans; they are powerful nonphysical intelligences.] (2 Cor. 11:14, 15, Revised Berkeley).

On November 14, 1976, the *San Francisco Examiner and Chronicle* carried a story reported by James Pearre of the *Chicago Tribune*. I think we will find it to be a most interesting piece of the puzzle. Those who doubt supernaturally induced experiences, intrusions into our world by some of the "hosts" that the Bible is talking about, might want to briefly examine a certain turning point in the world's history. Pearre wrote:

"Dr. Elisabeth Kubler-Ross, whose work has revolutionized attitudes about death and dying, says the spirit of a deceased former patient helped dissuade her nine years ago from abandoning her work . . . she since has become convinced that it was a 'spontaneous materialization of somebody who had died almost a year before.' Kubler-Ross discussed the mysterious incident reluctantly. She said her experience 'will sound so crazy that I wouldn't be surprised if people think, "Oh, she's now becoming an occultist, a spiritualist." ' " [1]

The incident occurred in her office at the University of

BEINGS OF LIGHT OR FALSE ANGELS OF LIGHT?

Chicago, where she was an associate professor of psychiatry. She had organized a series of seminars on death and dying, in which terminally ill patients discussed their innermost feelings about facing death.

A woman appeared at her office and introduced herself as a patient who had died ten months before, Kubler-Ross says. The visitor looked identical to the former patient, but Kubler-Ross refused to believe it could be the same person.

"She said she knew I was considering giving up my work with dying patients and that she came to tell me not to give it up," Kubler-Ross recalls. "She said the time was not right. I reached out to touch her. I was reality testing. I was a scientist, a psychiatrist, and I didn't believe in such things.

"I told her a white lie and said I wanted her to write a little note I could give to her minister. The minister and I had helped this woman a lot. This way, you know, I thought I could check her out by the handwriting.

"She smiled in this all-knowing way, like she knew very well what my intentions were." But the woman wrote the note and signed it, and handwriting analysis indicated that it matched the handwriting of the deceased patient.

Kubler-Ross says the incident "came at a crossroads where I would have made the wrong decision if I hadn't listened to her," and that her subsequent work has convinced her "there is life after death." Pearre then proceeds to quote Kubler-Ross's involvement with mediumism as a source of evidence of afterlife. She has even worked out a system so that her deceased patients can get in touch with her. That short visit has resounded around the world, almost starting a crusade for death and dying. As already has been pointed out, the real Pandora's box that has opened has been the emergence of occult doctrine on a greater scale than before.

Since that time, Kubler-Ross has gotten to know her spirit guide, Salem, well enough for him to materialize in her room. For those who understand spiritism, that signifies a very advanced involvement. Exactly what she has learned from Salem in the way of advanced teachings, I cannot say, but I have a good idea. Whereas she has not revealed publicly what Salem has shared with her (though he could be preparing her to do so), the teachings of other spirit guides, or beings of light, are available. A profound connection exists among every one of these "higher teachings," which is far from accidental; indeed, it is most intentional, most timely, for history's present course.

In order to be heard as a scientific voice, Moody has to keep a cautious neutral distance from too much dogma. The scientific presentation requires an air of detachment, but be assured that some of the most effective editorializing comes from who is selected to say what. Moody, a partner and friend of Kubler-Ross's, appears to be more the scientist. It is important to review a few of his discoveries before proceeding. We will see the beginnings of "higher teachings," which have paved the way for more advanced teachings. Again, when the public climate is right, there is every possibility that the spirit guide of Kubler-Ross will use her as a mouthpiece.

Reviewing the Moody material briefly, the following subject is a man who saw a small "ball of light" hovering in an upper corner of his hospital room. The patient is then quoted by Moody:

> I turned over and tried to get in a more comfortable position, but just at that moment a light appeared in the corner of the room, just below the ceiling. It was just a ball of light, almost like a globe, and it was not very large, I would say no more than twelve to fifteen inches in diameter, and as this light appeared, a feeling came over me. I can't say it was an eerie feeling, because it was not. . . . I could see a hand reach down for me from the light, and the light said, "Come with me. I want to show you something." So immediately, without any hesitation whatsoever, I reached up with my hand and grabbed onto the hand I saw. As I did, I had the feeling of being drawn up and of leaving my body, and I looked back and saw it lying there on the bed while I was going up towards the ceiling of the room.
>
> . . . I took on the same form as the light. I got the feeling, and I'll have to use my own words for it, . . . that this form was definitely a spirit. It wasn't a body, just a wisp of smoke or a vapor. It looked almost like the

clouds of cigarette smoke you can see when they are illuminated as they drift around a lamp. The form I took had colors, though. . . .

So, I was drawn up to the same position the light was in, and we started moving through the ceiling and the wall of the hospital room, into the corridor, and through the corridor, down through the floors it seemed, on down to a lower floor in the hospital.[2]

The patient and his spirit guide, as Moody relates in five pages of direct quotation, glide around and dialogue, the subject experiences feelings of great inner calm, and finally—like the classical magical wish—the being of light grants the patient a longer life. At the very least, this is an out-of-the-body experience combined with a spirit contact.

This episode is mediumistic by definition; it is as simple as that. The ensuing debate regarding the subject's willingness to participate in the experience, as opposed to his being a victim of something, is lengthy and complex. He himself says that without hesitation he extended his hand to the being. I am certain that he could have, or someone else would have, refrained. In some occult testimonies, people have prayed in fear and the presence left. Such has been true in my own life.

Moody tells of another interesting discovery: "In a few instances, people have come to believe that the beings they encountered were their 'guardian spirits.' One man was told by such a spirit that, 'I have helped you through this stage of your existence, but now I am going to turn you over to others.' A woman told me that as she was leaving her body she detected the presence of two other spiritual beings there, and that they identified themselves as her 'spiritual helpers.' " [3] Then Moody reports that a number of people have come out of these experiences with psychic abilities.[4]

One of Moody's subjects says, "You know in your heart there's no such thing as death. You just graduate from one thing to another—like from grammar school to high school, to college." Another testimony follows: "Life is like imprisonment. In this state, we just can't understand what prisons these bodies are. Death is such a release—like an escape from prison. That's the best thing I can think of to compare it to." [5]

In the next few paragraphs, Moody completes what the Bible missed; he corrects it where it errs. But invariably he reminds us of the standard biblical caricatures, so that they will stay in our minds as representations of Christianity, and then he indulges in two sweeping statements that seem to demolish the paper dummies he has erected. "No one has described the cartoonist's heaven of pearly gates, golden streets, and winged, harp-playing angels, nor a hell of flames and demons with pitchforks." [6] In place of this caricature, which has nothing to do with true biblical revelation, comes an erudite and fair-minded improvement. Moody goes on: "So in most cases, the reward-punishment model of the afterlife is abandoned and disavowed, even by many who had been accustomed to thinking in those terms. They found, much to their amazement, that even when their most apparently awful and sinful deeds were made manifest before the being of light, the being responded not with anger and rage, but rather only with understanding, and even with humor." [7]

The one thing that the perfect God of the Bible does not find amusing is human sin as it manifests itself across a great spectrum of cruelties, dehumanizations, perversities, and rank horrors. The living God of Scripture will not greet Himmler, Goebbels, or Hitler with cosmic giggles of amused understanding. That would be a miscarriage of justice to the mangled victims and would not be good. Such cosmic tolerance, the contented good-neighbor policy with evil, ultimately spells a topsy-turvy universe whose "god" is insane or evil. True goodness, as a quality of deity, must be absolute.

What higher or more sublime good replaces the biblical caricatures? "In place of this old model, many seemed to have returned with a new model and a new understanding of the world beyond—a vision which features not unilateral judgement but rather cooperative development [and here Moody lets the cat out of the bag] towards the *ultimate end of Self-realization.*" [8]

That is Eastern mysticism, with the identical "self-realization" propounded in *The Tibetan Book of the Dead*. It is the final reward given those who have maneuvered through the obstacle course of *bardos* ("death planes"), those who have come to know "their essential nature," those whose eyes have remained on the pelucid "clear light." That "self-realization" is *moksha;* it is *Nirvana* ("enlightenment"). It appears that Moody uses the term *self-realization* most deliberately, for he *has* cited *The Tibetan Book of the Dead,* where this term is crucial to its view of the cosmos, and it is consistent with reincarnationist views. It appears to be no accident that Moody mentions Dr. Ian Stevenson's *Twenty Cases Suggestive of Reincarnation* as further resource material (the same Ian Stevenson who tried to arrange séances with the "greatest medium of the century," Arthur Ford, and who has been in contact with the most famous medium in America today, Jane Roberts, through whom "Seth" speaks). When you annihilate Christianity, there is only one great religious alternative; it is pantheism, it is Hinduistic mysticism. That is what Moody is leaving us with, and that is invariably the emergent "gospel" of his subjects who have become spirit contacts. This pattern is almost infallibly consonant with every contact that a subject or medium has had with a spirit, which I have ever studied. Christian doctrines are either tampered with or annihilated.

Moody has opened the door. Although he has not given us the most significant information yet, he has told us a few key premises that lead to a definite place. We know that there is a higher plane of spirit, that there are spirits, that there are beings of light, that the whole scheme seems to be the evolution of the soul or self, and that many of these fascinating truths have come through people who have talked to beings of light or spirit guides.

Knowing all of this, if you and I should go on an excursion into the neighborhood drugstore or supermarket, we would be able to find on the average bookrack numerous "higher revelations," which have come through a recent host of spirit contacts. If we are persuaded that these beings of light are out there for our own good and that they are our cosmic allies—and if we have become convinced of them through reading Moody—it will behoove us to listen attentively to what they are saying.

One of these books, a major occult best seller, flooded the

bookracks three years ago, and it and several other books by the same author are still best sellers. Like an old enemy on a street corner, it drew my eyes in recognition as, well past midnight, I stared at the gnarled face of Jane Roberts emerging from a purple paperback cover, contorting like a vampire in a Polish horror film. She had been photographed while "Seth" was taking over her body. I squinted my eyes in thought and looked off. Recalling my era in Egyptology, I said to myself, "Seth is the name of the Egyptian god of evil." Sure enough, when I checked it out in Webster's dictionary, it said: "Seth, n. an Egyptian god represented as having the head of a beast and a pointed snout. He was the brother of Osiris and the personification of physical evil and darkness, the adversary of good."

With irony, I remarked to myself under my breath, "And this is what the modern age has sought after to replace God: the infallible pride of science and humanism, the smugness, the mockers who sneer at the clear sanity of biblical revelation and then go groping after something that is such a travesty that it makes consummate fools of them all."

The Apostle Paul, in the Epistle to the Romans, states the ironic justice that pursues the willfully blind: "For even though they knew God, they did not honor Him as God, or give thanks; but they became futile in their speculations, and their foolish heart was darkened. Professing to be wise, they became fools, and exchanged the glory of the incorruptible God for an image" (Rom. 1:21-23, NASB).

The face of the medium on the cover was a dead giveaway. A normal child would sense it, and recoil in horror; yet here was a best-selling book about a modern medium and the creature that used her body as a mouthpiece to the world. The book by Jane Roberts is entitled *Seth Speaks*.[9] Other books by Roberts would follow.

This is the drama that took place in the life of the modern medium, as recorded in *The Seth Material* by Roberts: The scenario is a liberated literary graduate of Skidmore University portrayed as an honest seeker of truth who convinces us that her ventures into the occult were innocent, natural, and in no way premeditated. She just happened to stumble over a Ouija board one day as her husband, out of the blue, recommended that she write a book on ESP. On the night of December 8, 1963, the Ouija board's pointer began to move. That was when the doorway opened and Seth entered their lives. The first messages were sufficiently profound, endearing, and casual to pull them in. The spirit was called "Frank Withers," of all innocuous names; a local dead man, so to speak. But soon it said that it preferred not to be called Frank Withers. When they asked what to call it, the reply was, "To God, all names are his name." Then it said, "You may call me whatever you choose. I call myself Seth, it fits the me of me."

After several sessions, Jane, the medium, began to anticipate the words in her mind before the pointer spelled them out on the Ouija board. In her description of the transition she says that the pointer paused, and she felt as if she were standing at the top of a high diving board. It was as if she were trying to make herself jump while people were waiting impatiently behind her. She took the leap, and for the first time she began to speak for Seth. The words continued the sentences the board had spelled out. The being acted like a jocular, wise, paternal old friend from some past life. Yet it made no mistake in showing that it was fully superhuman and, among other things, trying to get across to this world the wisdom that it was only now ready for.

With the innocent tone of a high school girl following a cooking recipe, Jane says that a séance was in order for her ESP book. So she went about setting up Christmas tree lights and making other preparations. She got her money's worth; Seth stunned them. He transmogrified her body. It wasn't exactly a thing of beauty, to be sure, but it was a supernatural intervention. Not a high-order miracle, mind you, but it was something. Those at the table were told by the voice to concentrate on Jane's arm. One witness, Robert Butts, said that the hand began to change in appearance and resembled a paw. It gave Butts a very eerie feeling. He said that the hand became stubby and fat for a moment. Then it resumed its pawlike appearance. Then Seth told him to reach out and touch the hand. Butts cautiously touched Jane's hand. It felt very cold, wet, and clammy, and seemed unusually bumpy. Then Seth made the whole forepaw glow.

But as if this gesture was not enough, Seth had another

trick. They faced a mirror and Seth told them to look at their reflections in the mirror. As they watched, Jane's image was replaced with another different image. The head dropped lower and the shape of the skull and the hair style changed. The head in the mirror leaned down although Jane was sitting erect, looking straight ahead. Naturally, it would take the three people a little while to acclimate themselves to such bizarre antics, but they would soon triumph and transcend their visceral horror.

The Seth sessions continued. The next breakthrough in the taking over of Jane's body was the appearance of a deep masculine voice, which issued from the medium's body. Seth told Jane's husband that he had been an extremely vain woman in a former life. Seth was also calling Jane "Ruburt," a male name. Then Seth commented philosophically that he feared that Jane would sound rather unmelodious as a man's voice.

Jane (now Ruburt) observed that they didn't realize they would receive what was known as the Seth material through the "psychic structure." She acknowledged a sense of great power in Seth's voice. It made her feel very small, as if surrounded by great energy. In time she would walk, gesture, and grimace while in a deep trance. She would even learn to sip wine occasionally as Seth spoke through her.

But there was an incident that almost ended the sessions. Jane, who by now had had a series of out-of-the-body experiences, said she was in her bedroom, and became suddenly aware of a dark, looming figure menacing her. She had not previously believed in demons, but changed her mind when the attacker dragged her around and even bit her hand. Finally the thing tried to kill her and she screamed.

Later, Seth would explain it all away. Naturally, it was merely a projection of her mind, the energy of hidden fears. Then Seth assured her and her husband (who took notes of everything the medium said) that the evil that "Ruburt" imagined did not exist.

Later, a fairly well-known psychologist interviewed Seth to see if it was a double personality. It was his opinion that Seth had a "massive intellect" and did not seem to be a secondary personality. Later this would be borne out clearly by a number of telepathic and clairvoyant tests, combined with the fact that the Seth creature would produce five thousand typewritten records and analogues of higher esoteric truth. Some of it was most subtle, indeed, but much of the teachings would be a redundant weaving of semantic spells, as Seth came out again and again with the same ideas in different words. Invariably it would be in abstract, often abstruse, erudite, elusive language, with as much scientific and technical jargon as possible.

In this aspect, and in many of the teachings, the Seth material would be very similar to the impersonal voice that spoke through the entranced Edgar Cayce. Only at the end of Cayce's life, according to private sources, did the medium suspect that it was a powerful being and not the universal mind, the "Akashic records." Cayce's books have filled the bookracks for twenty years, many of them best sellers for the past decade. He, like Arthur Ford, has been called "the greatest medium of the century."

But now back to Seth. Let's examine a number of these teachings. Jane Roberts reports on Seth's concept of God. Certain salient points of the description are:

1. God is not human, though he passed through human stages (and it is at this point that the Buddhist myth comes closest to approximating reality).

2. He is not a single individual, but an "energy gestalt."

3. This energy forms all the universes. Seth renames God "All That Is," as opposed to the "I Am That I Am" of the Holy Bible.

Creation, Seth says, was a massive dilemma for God and his one means of escape from cosmic insanity. This is exactly the opposite of the picture of joy, glory, and sovereignty of the biblical creation. In this case, "god" comes across as a huge tapeworm with a billion latent eggs. If the eggs do not spew out, the god will burst. The prototypes of creation, latent within its imagination, needed expression.

4. No personal God-individual exists, to use Christian terms. Human beings are cocreators, and what we call God is the sum of all consciousness, and yet the whole is more than the sum of its parts.

Seth stresses reincarnation time and again throughout the book, along with the God-is-within concept.

If some of this is beginning to sound like science fiction

with "Zonar Nine-Five" and "The folks from Astroid Twelve," or the U.S.S. *Enterprise* of "Star Trek" fame drifting along the cranial nerve of a billion-mile cretin, there is more to come. And this, I must admit, I find repugnant. If Frank Withers, the number-one spirit, was jettisoned and engulfed by Seth, something came along named Seth II, an ancient friend of Seth I, that gave Seth I a punt, as though he were a small soccer ball. (It reminds me of the cartoon of the ocean where the minnow is eaten by the bigger fish, and so on until the predator reaches the size of a sperm whale.) Seth II sounds like a large manta ray.

Ruburt (Alias Jane Roberts) tells what happened one night in April 1968 (the fifth year of the Seth sessions). By then Jane had been forbidden by Seth to read "religious books" and, as she confesses, she knew almost nothing about the Bible to begin with.

With massive power the voice started to break through, and Jane was hurled off into a void. The voice sounded clear though distant. Jane felt as if a cone had come down over her head. The voice claimed to come from an alien dimension, so alien that the contact was almost a miracle.

On June 8, the pyramid effect started again. Now it was plural, speaking of itself as "we." "They" described themselves as an entity which existed before our own time frame, and which was instrumental in forming energy into physical form.

Jane said that under this new Seth's influence, her body became like a puppet and her face expressionless.

After that visitation, Jane encountered difficulty getting back, and Seth had to help her.

When Jane went back into a trance, she had a trauma. Recently she had been not only the recipient of words, but of direct spiritual revelations and experiences as well. She says that the entity referred to individuals returning in the future to peer into physical reality like giants upon the floor. At that point she saw a giant's face peer into her living room, its face filling up the entire window. Then her body, the room, and its contents all grew to enormous size. She screamed and began to tremble violently.

Jane had one more bout with the higher Seth, but she

became so shaken that the regular Seth did not allow it to continue for a long time. Again she felt the "cone" above her head and saw the giant looking at her. At this point she struggled to get in touch with her vocal cords. She seems to have felt somewhat violated by the being, a problem she never felt with the lower Seth. All the same, the medium goes on to make excuses for it, saying that it did not understand from its heightened state that she found the experiences unpleasant.

The last statement from Seth II in the chapter is a godlike declaration. He (or "they") claimed to have given man the mental images from which man formed the known world and his own physical self.

A pluralistic entity taking over a man in the Bible is seen in the madman, the Gadarene, whose name was Legion. Christ could have hurled the demons into the abyss; but as an illustration of their concrete reality, he sent them into a large herd of pigs. Then the pigs charged into the sea and killed themselves. The man in his possessed state had exhibited a sufficient range of superhuman and paranormal feats to scare everyone away. Among other things, he had the physical strength to snap heavy chains. But when Christ appeared, the demons trembled in horror. Legion was demon-possessed.

What is Seth? It—they, the pluralistic entity—is a demon, a mediumistic demon. There is no reason to believe what it says, for it is a brilliant liar. This woman's Ouija board caught a spiritual manta ray, and she is too seduced by it to know it. Yet Roberts is only too accountable, for at a specific time in her life she turned her back on the God of the Bible. She refers to that era scornfully, making sure to give us the caricatures. She says that as she grew older she found it increasingly difficult to accept the God of her ancestors. God seemed to be as dead as they were. And here comes the caricature, as she asks somewhat rhetorically what kind of God would require constant adoration by subjects sitting around singing hymns. This woman, who claims to be intelligent, asks this on the one hand and confesses ignorance of the Bible on the other hand.

Roberts made her decision. She decided that that kind of God was out and she would not have him as her friend. She then observes that it appears that God had not treated his own Son very well.

In the place of the biblical God, this woman has chosen the one who bears the same name as the Egyptian god of evil, "Seth," the ancient twin of Osiris; Seth, whose image is carved in the dank, musty descending corridors of stone beneath the Valley of the Kings, whose huge stone colossuses lean against the bulbous pillars of Karnak, a subterranean god from the ancient past of Egypt. This multiple identity, Seth, claims to have never been enfleshed. Little wonder; this being from the void existed before the foundations of our world. It floated across the ancient world, for it is a spirit; it has always been a spirit. And there are others. We learn from the Apostle Paul that the originators and powers behind the ancient idols were "elemental spirits." In 1 Corinthians 10:19, 20 (Revised Berkeley), Paul says, "What then am I saying? That an offering to idols amounts to anything, or that the idol itself is anything? No, but that which they sacrifice, they are offering to *demons* and not to God" (italics added). This problem is reiterated in Deuteronomy 32:16, 17 (NASB) about the truth of idol worship: "They sacrificed to demons who were not God, to gods whom they have not known, new gods who came lately." Such is Seth.

Again Paul says, "But the Spirit [of God] explicitly says that in later times some will fall away from the faith, paying attention to deceitful spirits and doctrines of demons" (1 Tim. 4:1, NASB). So there is dire warning to those who are already Christians. What will be the means of spiritual seduction? Deceitful spirits. Incidentally, the word *demon*, from the Greek *daimon*, means "knowing" or "wise." Spirits have knowledge far beyond mere temporal mortals, and the fierce range of their superhuman powers emerges when one studies the Greek connotations of the following words: *principalities, powers, dominions*. Ephesians 6:12 says, "For we wrestle not against flesh and blood, but against principalities, against powers, against the rulers of the darkness of this world, against spiritual wickedness in high places." In the Revised Berkeley Version, the latter part of the verse reads, "the cosmic powers of this present darkness; against the spiritual forces of evil in the heavenly spheres."

If you decided to turn your back on the biblical God, entered into occult pursuits, emptied your mind, and surrendered to an invisible intelligence, to whom or what would you go? The clear answer is: to one of these above-named wicked potentates. Not Fred Jones, not Fletcher (the guide to Arthur Ford), or anybody else with some tame home-town name, but instead, *a demonic being*. The blanket warning that the Bible issues regarding all spirit contact now emerges as a profoundly sensible injunction. Should you care to gamble in this particular casino, the odds against you infinitely outweigh the grade schooler trying his luck at Caesar's Palace in Las Vegas.

The consensus of all evangelical Bible scholars, using clear exegesis, is that the deceased, the dead, cannot be contacted. God has created an impassable barrier. What are, in fact, being contacted in place of the sought-after human souls are some type of deceiving spirits masquerading as the deceased, some spirits out of the untold myriad for whom *Tehom* ("the abyss") was prepared before the foundations of our physical universe. The number of these spirits is great, this we know. A genius, humanly speaking, with a massive genealogical card file, encyclopedic memory, and an active imagination could fool most people at a séance. An immortal spirit with a superhuman intelligence would have no trouble fooling just about anybody who tried to engage it, especially if the contact, no matter how brilliant, disregarded the Bible. Men alone are no match for these things. Part of the "con" is to get people to believe that they are sufficiently armored with their own minds and intuitions. They are not. The Rand Think Tank is not, even if you throw in the faculty of M.I.T., Harvard, Stanford, and the Ivy League, even if you unified their minds. Unlike the baleful powers, none of these men was around to witness the creation of galaxies and atoms. The account of the role of the angelic hosts was that they saw, and in some way participated in, God's sovereign act of creation (they "shouted for joy," Job 38:7). Those among these creatures who would later oppose God, whose natures would twist, would still retain, in a perverted form, much of their intellect, power, and knowledge. What hideous strength they have!

Therefore, it makes sense, in the biblical tradition, for God to forbid spiritism. Anything else would not be love. If a host of cosmic beings once rebelled, then God knows of it and lovingly warns us of it. We have seen the numerous statements of Moody, Kubler-Ross, Cayce, Bishop Pike, Dowling, and Roberts. We have seen that there is an invisble world of beings—spirits—that some people can contact. We have seen their teachings, and the similarity of these teachings, and the obsession, common among all the teachings, with Jesus Christ. We also have seen the mainline spiritualistic and spiritistic views of the afterlife: that it is a progressive, multilayered, and multidimensional spirit plane where all souls evolve. The physical body is an unpleasant shell to be jettisoned. Real happiness, we are told, only begins on the other side. The biggest prize of all, we are then assured, is the ultimate stage of spiritual evolution where one becomes a being of light. We are asked to accept these statements on faith. It is that simple; this is a religion and its high priests are the mediums. To accept its view, we are forced to ignore the Bible and finally say, "The Bible is wrong." At that point, one has believed the spirits.

Finally, we are forced to ask, as God himself seeks to reason with his people, "And when they say to you, 'Consult the mediums and the wizards who whisper and mutter,' should not a people consult their God? Should they consult the dead on behalf of the living?" (Isa. 8:19, NASB).

SECTION THREE

DEATH IN THE EAST—YOGIS, MYSTICS, AND MYSTERY RELIGIONS

SIX
THE ANCIENT TRADITION: ITS HEART AND ESSENCE
*coauthored by
Brooks Alexander*

In the last two chapters we saw the strange tales of the psychics. It is evident that they have a whole range of experiences and are directly connected with the continuum of the ancient tradition. But, frankly, they are not as advanced as the yogis or Eastern masters. They are on the same path and hint at the same conclusions about existence; but, compared to accomplished yogis, they are still aspirants, at times operating on a first-grade level. The accounts of India's most "evolved" yogis, such as Ramakrishna, Aurobindo, or Yogananda, reveal that their most elementary spiritual experiences begin where many of our psychics are now, and they soon go far beyond them. Yogis are linked directly, traditionally, and historically with the ancient tradition, having systematized and perfected this tradition for centuries. Their astral travels end when they are spiritual teenagers, for they are shooting for the "big one" and are not interested in any small-time "food tasting in pastel planes," which "look just like earth." A yogi sneers at that kind of activity. He shoots "beyond the seven planes, and beyond the seven shakras, to what they all call *samadhi*." *Samadhi* ("a state of deep concentration which results in union with ultimate reality") is the biggest death experience of all.

Let's not hide our eyes, for America also has started to chase the "big one." In ten years, the countercultural daydream of a society unified around the experience of "the divine within" has become a concrete reality. It goes far beyond the fringe groups on which the media reports. Indeed, mystical doctrines have influenced wide areas such as science, commerce, politics, the arts, and psychology, as well as religion. The basic ideas about man, meaning, and God that are inherent in the ancient tradition are showing up as root premises in all sorts of contemporary trends. TV and movies, from "Kung Fu" to "Close Encounters of the Third Kind," harp on them all day long.

This new-age occultism in America is a kind of "cosmic humanism." But it is tapped directly from the big conduit of the ancient tradition with its "hidden wisdom," so inherent to the Eastern path. This means that people at every level of today's culture are being conditioned to accept a definition of reality which ultimately denies the personal God of the Bible; asserts the autonomy, power, and inherent divinity of man; and condemns as obsolete any absolute statements of moral values.

C. S. Lewis offers insight into what is happening: "Pantheism ['all-is-one'] is congenial to our minds not because it is the final stage in a slow process of enlightenment, but because it is almost as old as we are. It may even be the most primitive of all religions. It is immemorial in India. The Greeks rose above it only at their peak . . . their successors lapsed into the great pantheistic system of the Stoics. Modern Europe escaped it only while she remained predominantly Christian: with Giordano, Bruno, and Spinoza it returned. With Hegel it became almost the agreed philosophy of highly educated people. . . . So far from being the final religious refinement, pantheism is in fact the permanent natural bent of the human mind; the permanent ordinary level below which man sometimes sinks, but above which his own unaided efforts can never raise him for very long. It is the attitude into which the human mind automatically falls when left to itself. No wonder we find it congenial. If "religion" means simply what man says about God, and not what God does about man, then pantheism almost is religion. And religion in that sense has, in the long run, only one really formidable opponent—namely, Christianity."[1]

THE ANCIENT TRADITION

In the meantime, the spiritual anemia of the West has left this generation ravenous for reality, and therefore vulnerable to any "spiritual" novelty offered in the name of truth.

But let us look at the heart of the ancient tradition. The traditional systems of occult, mystical, and Eastern philosophy are patterned after the archetypal lie of Genesis 3. Although intellectual constructions, they are intermingled, in the first instance, with a rare strain of reported experiences, the experiences of "cosmic totality." The *Upanishads* report that a drug known as "soma" was used to ignite some of the mystical experiences of the rishis. Likewise, someone sitting on a hill today eating peyote bulbs would typically give an experiential report that the stars, sky, trees, and all existence felt as though a unifying current of energy were holding it all together, and therefore *that* was the fundamental reality. The mystical systems that seek to interpret this experience can be analyzed into a number of related categories of thought. The four central presuppositions are:

1. *All is one.* Someone has a unitive experience. The effect is to dissolve all distinctions (the perceiver and the objects perceived) into a single, undifferentiated unity. This is where we obtain the first presupposition of monistic philosophy: there is only one reality in existence. From this, it follows that all apparent separations and oppositions (good and evil) are illusory manifestations of the single divine reality. All objects and individuals are merely parts of the all-inclusive one. The Hindus call it *atma-paramatma*, *Brahman*, and *sat-chit-ananda* ("being-consciousness bliss").

Nobel physicist Erwin Schrodinger said that his world view was derived from Vedanta and that ultimately there is only a single consciousness. "The external world and consciousness are one and the same thing, in so far as both are constituted by the same primitive elements."[2]

2. *Man is a divine being within.* If there is only a single reality in existence, then we are obviously parts or emanations of it. Our own "consciousness" provides the specific connecting link. In experiencing this reality, we experience our oneness with the "divine," as well as the essential divinity of our

innermost nature. All forms of occult philosophy are united around the central belief that the inner or real self of man is God. This is the fundamental form of the primary lie spoken of in Genesis, "You will be like God" (Gen. 3:5, RSV).

3. *Life's purpose is to realize the divine within.* No matter how the "divinity" of man may be defined by a particular path or subtradition, the "way" is usually the path of supreme illumination or *gnosis* ("the attainment of supreme knowledge"). Other mystical terms for it are *enlightenment, samadhi, at-one-ment, Nirvana, self-realization, satori,* and *God-consciousness.* This state of gnosis is usually reached by spiritual and psychic techniques, such as raja or kundalini yoga. Thus, the yogi finds union within the divine principle. The idea is that the person is a cosmic amnesiac who has forgotten his true divine identity, but the right system will remind him that he is really God after all. The closer he is to becoming God, the more conscious he becomes. The advanced yogi can supposedly remember back thousands of lifetimes which he has passed. He is seeking eternal death in order to extinguish himself from the painful round of rebirths, so death of his identity is required before he can wake up and become God. Thus, he is on a personal, subjective, and experiential trip and must discard any reliance which comes from the outside—faith, revelation, and information to the contrary.

4. *Self-realization leads to psycho-spiritual power.* This is where Uri Geller, Sai Baba, and Bubba Free John are, and where Walt Disney obtained his occult tales of "The Sorcerer's Apprentice." Things materialize and dematerialize, tables float, yogis levitate, and psychics see what is happening a hundred miles away.

As an initiate advances upon the path of gnosis, he becomes increasingly familiar with the divine "one" and its relationship to the phenomenal world of reality, "creation." Thus, he, as man-God, alledgedly becomes master and creator of his own reality. Through his knowledge and utilization of ultimate laws, according to the rationale, he becomes capable of creating and manipulating his environment or that of others. (Disciples often interpret dramatic events as direct intercessions of their gurus intervening in time-space.) Inasmuch as reality is supposedly composed of consciousness, the adept learns to control reality by controlling consciousness; matter is created or dematerialized with the facility of a divine conjurer.

It is here that mysticism merges into magic and vice versa. The palpable excuse for the magic miracle is pantheism, and the miracle might even be offered as proof that the consciousness of man can ascend to a level where it can control matter and events in a godlike manner. But the other way of interpreting this is that the man, not by an innate power, but by surrendering to an outside spiritual agency, is acting as a circuit through which the spirit power can manifest itself. Uri Geller, on a BBC talk show, claimed that he received his power to bend nails by looking at them from a number of "cosmic intelligences" that channeled through him.

The fact remains that if any path, religion, or tradition includes even one of the four points mentioned above, it is certain that the thrust of its teaching runs counter to authentic Christianity. In the ancient tradition, man becomes God. In the Bible, that proposition is the ultimate lie. Man enters blissful communion with God through Christ alone, but he never becomes what he is not: God. Can a buffalo become a U. S. Congressman? Only if you believe in reincarnation. But nobody can prove it. Otherwise we would agree that the buffalo belongs in a field. India has tried placing the cow in positions of high office, and the results have been preposterous.

By simple logic alone, the main principles of the pantheistic system of man becoming God are: reincarnation, karma (the law that determines the level of birth), the belief that physical matter is maya (an illusion), and the methods of escape—yoga, meditation, idolatry, the mystery religions, the guru system, the techniques of astrology and tarot, special diets, drugs, and all manner of consciousness-expansion techniques to realize the "supreme identity."

But do these things help someone realize his godhood, or are they merely elaborate techniques for brainwashing him into finally swallowing whole that which a main part of him, his conscience, testifies against? Part of yoga's surgery is to kill the conscience, because a dead conscience makes becoming God much easier; there are no longer any squawks from the person's protesting conscience, which denies that he is God!

Where do all these paths lead? To death, the final exit—death of the ego, death of the personality, death of the will, death of all desires, death of the intellect, and ultimate death to living and to life. That is *moksha*. The ancient tradition says, "Die and you will be free." It has to work that way. If a person is not who he is, then his present personality has to be destroyed, because it is getting in the way of his finding out who he is.

The master prize of the yogis is *turya samadhi* ("supreme enlightenment"). Most of the religious writings of India's gurus speak about it. If it is reached, the yogi loses all desire to live; he does not eat or sleep, and after twenty-one days he dies. They say he is dead forever.

But let us leave "religion" for a second and look at the problem from man's viewpoint. Everybody has to deal with death, and there are only so many options one can select.

Just as death is final and total separation from the world we are so used to, so the awareness of that end shatters our attempt to find some sense or value to life in the here and now. A man sweating away on death row can hardly taste a lobster dinner if his mind is doing mental replays of the electric chair. Those who contemplate death while alive know that the show will be over sooner than they think; their house and property and friends will be taken away. If you feel uneasy when going away from your hometown with friends, then going alone to Chicago can unsettle you. But the trip to Chicago is only for a week or two, and you know exactly what you have to come back to. You may never come back from death, and you have nowhere to go. All the people and things on which you have leaned for so long will not go with you. Let's be honest. In some hidden recess of your mind, death is the ultimate terror. It can haunt you with fear.

All "religion" ultimately is an attempt to come to terms with the pervasive and insidious fragmentation of our lives, which is introduced by the prospect of certain death. Humanity cannot escape a "religious" response to its condition, because individuals can never escape the fact that they must die. Specifically, this religious response is a groping for some ground of unity that will enable us to grasp an unknown harmony beyond the brittle disintegration of meaning which fractures all of our present hope and pleasures.

But the available grounds for unity are strictly limited. Those who seek unification of broken reality must find it either in the living, personal, and transcendent God who speaks the cosmos into existence purposefully, or in some impersonal substrate of "being" which underlies the primordial duality of matter and energy.[3] Thus, the religious desire for unity has two options for fulfillment: transcendence through Christ to contact with the eternal, holy God, or "sub-scendence" through mystical self-awareness to contact with the void.

To speak of God and his creation is to exhaust the scope of reality and existence. There is nothing else. Everything that exists is either God himself or is created by him. This leaves an open door for mystical religions and occult philosophies to take an extra step and say, "It's all God, and so am I." In effect, if you do not seek communion in the true transcendent God, you inevitably turn to some aspect of creation, the void, and call that God. After all, the Egyptians worshiped the sun, the Chaldeans the stars, and Hindus will enshrine almost anything. Since the creation itself is "fallen" (Rom. 8:19-23), the biblical conclusion is that mysticism declares the way by which one embraces the fulfillment of the curse of the fall here and now.

To really make this graphic, let us examine the fruits of death in the East.

SEVEN
DYING IN INDIA: THE SYMPTOMS OF THE ANCIENT TRADITION

Many have been intrigued, their imaginations often running wild, by talk of the hidden teachings of the ancient tradition. Herman Hess wrote *Siddhartha*, which probably did more for the Indian tourist board than any intensive tourism campaign. But a question we are all burning to ask is, If the Eastern system of metaphysics is really the highest, what utopian side effects can we look for? What practical, real-life results can we see? A key criterion for weighing the truth Christ offers is, "By their fruits ye shall know them" (Matt. 7:20). By their deeds, personalities, and characters, you receive an indication of what lies within men's hearts. If there is deceit, either willful or self-deceptive, the stench will eventually find a way to escape. If man really is God, as some cultures state, how does he fare in day-to-day living? Does he have dignity, or does obscene and ignoble treatment belie the soporific falsehood? Finally, how does he approach death? Is it a joyous event? Are true hope and conquest in the eyes of the dying, and do yogis communicate this when they die? Are the common people champions of their great spiritual heritage?

First of all, it is no secret that magazines such as *Life, Look, Atlantic Monthly, Newsweek, Time, U.S. News & World Report,* and *National Geographic* usually have spoken of India with abject horror regarding conditions there. For the past decade we have read of famine, floods, pestilences, disease, massive overcrowding, political corruption, and specific symptoms within the masses of people, which indicate why some of these conditions got out of hand. Natural conditions are inevitable, but many reporters also have tied attitudes and thought patterns to India's immense social problems: such things as caste, idolatry, ritual ignorance and superstition, stoical indifference, passivity, and ultimate resignation to the powers of fate. One of the most brilliant films portraying the thousands of facets of India was made by a number of Frenchmen who smuggled their cameras into India and literally covered the land. Entitled *Phantom India*, it comprises eight parts of forty minutes each. Since the government of India and the Indians in general are hypersensitive about their self-image, and since the movie is unflattering, the Frenchmen are now *persona non grata* in India. Journalists who apply for visas are usually grilled suspiciously.

All of us are in love with the Eastern panorama of Himalayan waterfalls, Kashmiri lakes, Goan sea views, and tropical mango forests which we hear about occasionally. But as I found when I saw those places, and liked them, too many other things kept me from peace. For instance, they do not blot out the train ride from Rishikesh to Madras. Even while standing at some of India's key vistas, one senses an underlying feeling of poverty and desolation.

The truth is, I went to India all primed for the land of romanticized images which I had envisioned. But what I saw appalled me. Was I prejudiced? To the contrary, I had pursued Eastern metaphysics, yoga, and Vedanta for ten years before going. After the swami at the Ramakrishna Mission in London spent two hours grilling me, he concluded that my wisdom and understanding of Advaita and Vedantic philosophy were far beyond my years, even for an orthodox Brahmin let alone a Westerner. Years later he read a book I wrote while in India after being a foremost disciple of India's highest-ranking miracle-working guru, Sathya Sai Baba, and declared it "flawless in advaitic doctrine" (I canceled the book, *The Amazing Advent*, on the day it came out.[1])

If the Hindu belief system which I followed was true, if anything, it should have prepared me for the culture shock I experienced, as should have the four and a half years which I had spent as a teenager in the Arab world. But I still suffered culture shock. Something was happening there that made me ask, "Are these people really right? Do they have the truth? Or are they the most lost and deluded people on earth?" After all, they were the ones who carried the legacy of the great Eastern tradition, whose culture was a laboratory, a vast social experiment, on what happens when you spend thousands of years en masse, living by what might be the highest mystical and spiritual principles on earth.

But then I heard of some of the Hindu customs, for example, *sutee*, which is when the husband dies and his wife is thrown on the cremation fire with his body and belongings. Then there is something which I call the fish-bait phenomenon. An eyewitness described it: "One of the gods in a village temple will tell the priest that it is time for another sacrifice, and the god tells him who the victim will be. So the village teams up, goes to the guy with something like a huge fish pole, and baits his skin, running the entire length of his back, on something that resembles a massive fishhook. Then they go trotting around the village with the fellow hanging in agony from the fish pole." You can still see the scars today of the few who have survived this torture in order to appease some god. In the main, the British stamped out these two practices and others like them, but they still make one consider the origin of the ideas, as well as a system that can so readily absorb and justify them.

I know that we can talk about the Inquisition, the horrors and cruelties, and how that seems to invalidate the Christian Church. But the practices of the Inquisition could not have come from true followers of Christ, since they violate the letter and spirit of written Scripture; and only those whose lives conform to the criterion spoken of in the Bible can be defined as being truly of Christ. At the same time, I know that the two extreme examples mentioned above would be disavowed by numerous Hindu sects, though not all, and differing groups could find variant holy writings to support either position in India. But none can deny the idolatry, none can deny the yogic tortures, penances, pilgrimages, odd food habits, and other things which are found to be consistent with

Hindu revelation and the self-evolutionary concept of the East.

So the question remains: How is death approached by the masses, and how does the common man fare?

The answer is this: Indians live just to die. Death is the great release, and preparations are made for it from the moment of birth. Because of this, the land is full of machinations and rituals which anticipate and prepare for death. In that sense, it begins to resemble a spiritual Las Vegas, for death is the one big chance to pull the one-armed bandit on the wheel of rebirths and pop into the body of a king or a peasant the next time around.

The idea is to go into death with the right frame of mind, for that will help determine where one goes. It is the same idea that some use to approach an LSD experience: one's preparation, or "set," determines what happens. A whole gamut of ideas exists on the best way to prepare; these ideas or techniques constitute the whole system of yoga, for they prepare one for ego death and physical death. *The Tibetan Book of the Dead* is a manual on different ways to enter death, while the Hindu mainstay, *The Bhagavad Gita*, enumerates various ways to die, all of which have become the great schools of yoga.

In *The Bhagavad Gita*, for example, one of yoga's main schools stemmed from a statement made by Krishna, the Pan-like god-man avatar of the Hindus, considered a divine embodiment of Vishnu (the preserver in the Hindu pantheon). Krishna looked at his disciple, Arjuna, telling him a method of liberation: "Verily this divine illusion of mine [the universe], made up of the gunas [inert substance, active substance, and pure substance], is hard to surmount; but those who take refuge in me alone, they cross over this illusion."[2] Krishna had previously told Arjuna that he (Krishna) is God, that he created the universe, and that only those who worship him can escape. The path of yoga that this created is known as *bhakti marga*, "the path of devotion." The aspirant literally consecrates his life to a given deity, building shrines to it, thinking of it constantly, and abiding in its name. That is the path through which the yogi seeks liberation.

Another statement made by Krishna is: "Whatever a man

thinks of at the last moment when he leaves his body, that alone does he attain, O Kaunteya, being ever absorbed in the thought thereof."[3] From this statement have come numerous yoga schools geared to controlling the mind, clearing it out, and preparing by "right thinking" for the inevitable death journey. *Vichara Atma* ("Who am I?"), the yoga of unending self-inquiry, utilizes this. *Jnana Yoga*, "the path of intelligent discrimination," also is partly based on this verse, as are such yogas as *Dhyana*, "mind-clearing concentration," and *Mantra Yoga*, the yoga of continually repeating the name of a given god until if death should catch one unawares, the name of that god is on the lips. This is one reason why some yogis are rapt in concentration, unmoving for hours and oblivious of the outside world.

Again Krishna tells Arjuna, "The omniscient, the ancient, the ruler, minuter than an atom, the supporter of all, of form inconceivable, effulgent like the sun, and beyond all darkness [the impersonal Brahman godhead, i.e., Krishna's true condition as he claimed]; he who meditates on this resplendent supreme Purusha, at the time of Death, with a steady mind, devotion and strength of yoga, well fixing the entire prana [life force] in the middle of the eyebrows, he reaches Him."[4] The stakes are big here, for the promise is of the yogi reaching union with God. Later Krishna says that he becomes God because his *atma* ("true self") is one and the same as God.

Yoga is not really a means of appropriating grace. Rather, it is usually considered a high-powered method of shortcutting the agonizingly long course of "evolution" which the soul takes before liberation. This is the jackpot referred to earlier. Even the *bhakti marga* path of devotion is contingent on the self-help method, because the aspirant still must work up the constant fury of adoration which is necessary to release him. In the end, it works out anyway, because only the aspirant who is so pure, so evolved (the result of millions of meritorious lifetimes), has the kind of *sathwic* ("pure") heart that puts him in this category. To reach the stage of being a proper *bhakta* ("Hindu religious devotee") takes millions of lifetimes. Certain gurus talk about grace, but the belief system of an impersonal monistic reality denies it. The static eternal cannot give grace; it just is, and it is no more concerned about striving, suffering humanity than you or I lose sleep over the sight of rain washing ants off a tree trunk.

To accrue merit, millions of pilgrims swarm the humid ghats of Benares overlooking the Ganges River. The old, decrepit, infirm, and maimed will wait for the hour of death to plunge into the river, for they believe the river bathes the locks of Siva, the god of destruction, who supposedly sits at the base of the Himalayas. Some of their epics tell them all sorts of magical things about the Ganges River. The reality, though, is not romantic; it is sickening.

What the pilgrims are looking for is a cosmic loophole which will magically erase the endless skein of "karmic debt" they have accumulated over myriad lives. These are the merciless records that form the balance sheet of every individual, spanning from his earliest appearance in the universe as a primitive geode to his present lifetime. These records totally ordain his fate.

The law of Karma ties a pilgrim to the agonies of birth after birth, saying he will not ever escape until he can lead a perfect life. Someone who has led a mediocre life, unable to rise above the paltriness of a rock breaker, has the grim prospect of coming back no higher than his present life. He believes he will be jammed back in the next birth into some crowded family of peasants. His fear is that an unaccounted sin, something he did as a child, will weigh him down on the death plane, forcing him to a far lower station in life than he expected. The out-and-out criminal has nothing to look forward to but a general dread of the unknown. He might be reborn as a mange-covered dog, and it may take millions of lives to work his way back from there to his present position. This is enough to make some people whimper in anguish, and they do.

Even the man of virtue has no easy prospect ahead. His pilgrimage road to immortality and perfection still winds ahead for an eternity, with perhaps millions of more lifetimes to go through. And just one little life of error, or one indulgence too many, will cast him back eons of time to some ignoble body. That is why the Hindu kisses the feet of the guru. Still, the long search for "grace" is something of a gamble, and the seeker does not really know the results of his life until he has died. Then maybe he can find out whether a propitiatory ceremony in some remote little temple sufficiently appeased the cosmic powers to elevate his fate. The Hindu theology of grace is complex and baffling (remember, it cannot really exist).

What is the length of time that it takes a soul to end the hellish struggle for liberation? One of the most famous examples is from the lips of Krishna: as long as it takes a bird to utterly level the massive twenty-nine-thousand-foot slope of Mount Everest at the rate of one meager peck a year. Now think of being a coolie in Calcutta, or a tree snake—or who knows what else—for at least nine-tenths of that time. This prospect motivates people to do all kinds of extreme things. The formal term for this "day and night of Brahma" is *kalpa*. But even when one has finally entered the impersonal godhead, there is still the indubitable fact of the reoccurrence of the whole cycle of creation. It is eternal, going in and out of Brahman.

That great speedway of escape, yoga, can backfire too. The more high-powered it is, the more it can derail a person. The very ego that the initiate is trying to destroy can twist around and come back as a misshapen monster. Stories abound of yogis making large-scale goofs, reminiscent of the Dr. Jekyll and Mr. Hyde story, and loosing upon society some parapsychic freak who is misusing his powers. The *Kriya yogis*, *Kundalini yogis*, and *Raja yogis* have such great power that it is as if they are riding bareback on huge intercontinental missiles.

To sum it up pictorially, we can turn to Rishikesh, a Himalayan hill station, for a glimpse of where the yogic merit system leads. (I used to think of it as a spiritual Coney Island.) Rishikesh sprawls along the Ganges, nestled between two rising hill slopes. The Ganges is still clear there, closer to its source of melting Himalayan glacial ice, hundreds of miles before it transforms into the opaque stench that washes the ghats of Benares. Yogic and monastic orders fan out from the cluttered town and polka-dot the hills and mountains on both sides of the sacred river. Typical of Indian holy spots, it swarms continually with pilgrims. The stench of incense, cow dung, urine, and garbage fills the air. Bazaars full of trinkets, gods, and holy items wind through the town between wooden tea stalls and vegetarian restaurants, which are glorified shacks always surrounded by crippled and mangy dogs. The dirty, fiery hot food is practically inedible. When I stayed there I could seldom sleep because of continual street pandemonium and the religious festivals which went on night after night for one of the thousands of gods; firecrackers exploded, and loudspeakers blared with speeches, *bhajans* ("songs"), and dramas.

Outside of Rishikesh, pilgrims drift along the road with sacred cows, going from one temple to another. They range from the austere Shaivite sadhus wearing loincloths and saffron shawls, covered with ash, their knotted hair caked with cow dung, to ordinary citizens. Street gurus and *pandits* ("wise or learned men") give discourses to collections of passersby and beggars, who line up on the street with their begging bowls in front of them. Not too far off are the leper colonies.

Farther away are the hidden and fortressed *ashrams* ("secluded dwellings or retreats"), ranging from the Sivananda divine-life ashram to the newly built "Shankaracharya Nagar," Maharishi's academy of meditation, which is surrounded by a barbed wire fence, and where its nonhippy Western entrants are checked like CIA employees. It has auditoriums, lecture halls, dormitories, wooden cabins, and closed-circuit TV. It also has the highest initiation fee in town.

But at the base of the verdant mountain, across the river from Rishikesh, perhaps serving as a statement of the ancient origins of transcendental meditation and all the other schools of yoga, wind labyrinthine shrines, holy gardens, and temples housing gaudy and strange idols. To fully communicate the effect, here is my initial reaction, recorded years ago:

> The temples interconnected with weird gates, entrances, and hallways were painted in ghastly bright pastels that highlighted their otherworldly shapes. The most unhinging section of all was a temple with a courtyard of huge cement lotuses and figures that portrayed scenes out of the Hindu epics. Above the main pathway to the entrance, elevated glass cases protruded

from the walls which contained lifesized manikins of the main Hindu gods, clothed, four-armed, blue-black, with enigmatic death-mask expressions that either stared far off or right down at you through either two or four perfect glass eyes.

On every trek to the ashram they confronted me from their elevated dusty cases, and I inevitably wondered what state of mind a man would have to be in to see them as divine. Certainly the smell of cotton candy, salt-water taffy, combined with the sickly burblings of a Wurlitzer organ would end my ambivalence. But for now, there was always the possibility that I was hung up by "cultural variables." Their system would say that for every man there is a unique way of approaching the absolute. Yet why did these temples not generate a feeling of exuberance or sanctity, but rather of voidness, desolation, and death? And if this feeling was a sample of what the *rishis* called *Nirvana*, and should *Nirvana* be an absolute increase of this force, then perhaps it was the most terrible cosmic insanity conceivable.[5]

The effect of those sights is like that of a giant hundred-foot cement ice-cream cone, spray painted metallic purple and green, serving as a lure of the great worlds to meet the pilgrim after death.

Those who are on the road to paradise fight their fates like dung beetles forever rolling balls. Every aspirant is a thin and weatherbeaten island unto himself. All forms of austerity and discipline are witnessed, from the quiet ascetic sitting motionless for years, fed by passersby, to the desperate groans and chants of sadhus repeating a single *mantra* ("holy word") again and again all day, day in and day out. Occasionally one sees the path of true mortification: sun gazers who are blind from looking at the sun over the years, or those whose arms are still raised, wispy and atrophied, due to their constantly holding them up in some freeze position. Always there are the wandering ash-covered Shaivite sadhus ("renunciants, followers of Siva") carrying a trident, wearing radhraksha beads, frequently sitting on a little mat under a sun umbrella, and often smoking *ganga* ("hashish").

DYING IN INDIA

Then there are the peculiar *tapas* ("purifying disciplines") of each *ashramic* ("monastic") order, with each guru teaching a devoted band of followers his own brand of enlightenment: odd diets, yogic postures, power breathing *(pranayama)*, chanting for eighteen hours at a stretch to the accompaniment of cymbals and drums, fasting, going without sleep, bowing and posturing to shrines and particular deities, and all manner of physical hardship and denial. As one might expect, there is really not a great deal of exuberance and joy around the town of Rishikesh, no matter what anybody says.

Then, what of Tibet and Nepal? After all, they are Buddhist. Here is one more illustration of the bondage of the merit system as a means of facing death. In Lhasa and Kathmandu, neighboring India's borders, untold numbers of people can be found madly spinning what might look like toys, but what are actually prayer wheels. They save the people from having to utter a mantra for each spin, and do the work for them. Some people look quite frenetic as they spin away, obviously intent on chalking up a great deal of merit. Prayer wheels differ in size, rotation speed, and numbers of mantras within them. A few of the people in the merchant class are the real "pinball wizards," for they have electric fans with huge blades upon which are written thousands of names of gods. At so many RPMs per hour, the totals on the mantric scoreboard are uncountable. I will avoid the obvious detailed progression, merely mentioning the great potential of vast electromagnetic centrifuges containing billions of names of a god by the use of microphotography. *The Tibetan Book of the Dead* teaches essentially the same thing as Krishna said about repeating the name of a god.

Solomon and the prophets of Israel, in speaking of pagan ritual and idolatry, dismissed them as terminal futility and blasphemy. The pagans who did such things were portrayed as making monkeys of themselves. Paul the apostle claimed that such people were in bondage to demons.

Finally, what would make some intelligent people stoop to such acts? A most sophisticated, subtle, and palpable lie. The very concepts of mystical philosophy were certainly potent enough in my life to cause me to do any number of things. It takes a most thoroughly seduced intelligent man to bow before a stone image, while a peasant will do it without a moment's thought. That is why most of India at one time or another bows before some formidable stone god. This is the hundred-foot cement ice-cream cone! The Bible declares it, the philosophy, the idols, and the acts to be abominations. Who wants to go into death deceived?

Where did it all start? Who first had the idea that death is the ultimate release and that to prepare for it one must perform a lot of mumbo jumbo? We are coming to that.

EIGHT
DEATH IN BABYLON

For those who seek to understand it, death is a highly creative force. The highest spiritual values of life can originate from the thoughts and study of death. . . . It's not just a question of good and evil, heaven or hell, as you will see when you read the selection on Hinduism and Buddhism.

In the decades to come we may see one universe, one humankind, one religion that unites us all in a peaceful world.[1]

Elisabeth Kubler-Ross

Having just looked at the giant sprawling amoeba of Eastern mysticism gathering everything but true Christianity into itself, we now need to understand why the Bible predicts that in the last days an Eastern religion known as "Mystery Babylon" will be the reigning religion of the world. The Book of Revelation in the Bible emphatically speaks of a one-world religion and refers to it as "an abomination." Under its banner will be the diverse occult practices justified by the divine-within concept, those same arts practiced by Babylon of old. It will be a mystery religion, awesome in its subtlety. Yet the living God of the Bible shall declare war upon it and consume it in judgment.

The "mystery of iniquity," according to Paul the apostle, is the dynamic of why one man would embrace the final unitive counterfeit religion and why another man would shun it. People are accountable deep within themselves, and God alone shall completely reveal the secret of choice, says the Bible.

If we are to understand that Mystery Babylon is to become a world system (as the Bible predicts, replacing Christianity), it is important to know two things. We must appreciate what the Babylon of old embodied, and we must be able to pick out the present building blocks that will form the coming religion's system of Mystery Babylon. It is my contention that one of these building blocks is the doctrine on death arising out of the "breakthroughs" by recent thanatologists such as Moody and Kubler-Ross. Since the Kubler-Ross plan of afterlife is pantheistic, the stage is set for further progress toward the unitive system, for death can be another hub around which all the world religions can be forced to merge.

Let us examine Babylon of old. One of the greatest historical records is found in the Bible, which says that Babylon sinned; it missed the mark. The Hebrew word for "sin," *chatha*, means "go wide of the mark," which can mean to miss it by only a hair. But, in its essence, sin is a constant preference for the assertions or intuitions of self over the proclamations of God. In Babylon's case, its root sin was its "secret knowledge," which God abhorred.

Brooks Alexander, director of the Spiritual Counterfeits Project in Berkeley, California, reports:

> The precise nature of this secret knowledge is indicated by the mention of Babylon. In the Old Testament, Babylon was the persistent enemy of God and of God's people, both spiritually and politically. The city personified the continuous pressure of false religion against the redemptive designs of God. In chapter 47 of Isaiah we see God's scathing condemnation of Babylon's spiritual corruption.
>
> The context is especially important. We should notice that the preceding four chapters are placed as a deliberate contrast to the unveiling of the Babylonian error. Through Isaiah, God makes an overpowering revelation about himself. The keynote of this tremen-

dous self-disclosure is the phrase, "I AM." The pivotal assertion, "I AM THE LORD . . ." is in fact repeated 21 times in Isaiah 42.

The climax of God's self-description is reached in Isaiah 45:18—"I am the Lord, and there is no other . . . I did not say to the offspring of Jacob, 'Seek me in chaos' [or "the void"]. I the Lord speak the truth, I declare what is right."

From the peak of that pure, clear divine statement, it is a downhill slide to chapter 47. There God evaluates the spiritual realities behind the facade of the Babylonian religion. He strips bare the shameful deceit of her "wisdom."—"Now therefore hear this, you lover of pleasures, who sit securely, who say in your heart, 'I am, and there is no one besides me' . . . [judgment] . . . shall come to you in a moment . . . shall come upon you in full measure, in spite of your many sorceries and the great power of your enchantments. You felt secure in your wickedness, you said, 'No one sees me'; your wisdom and your knowledge led you astray, and you said in your heart, 'I am, and there is no one besides me' " (Isaiah 47:8-10).

The meaning of this could not be clearer. Babylon was condemned because its religion was based upon an illegitimate usurpation of divinity, an idolatrous identification of the human self with God.

We should not mistakenly assume that this unsparing denunciation is directed merely against the self-glorification of man's limited ego, the 'social self' or 'biographical identity' of the individual. A much more radical presumption is in view here. Secular history confirms for us that the distinguishing mark of the Babylonians was their cosmic view of man's nature. Historically speaking, the entire Chaldean culture, Babylon included, is known to have been deeply rooted in the esoteric science of astrology. Every aspect of this ancient civilization, its rule as well as its ritual, was charged with the power of its occult symbology and the secret wisdom of its priestly initiates.

The most significant religious edifice in Babylon was

the Ziggurat, which in addition to serving as an astrological observatory was an astral temple symbolically representing the structure of reality. The Ziggurat as the "cosmic mountain" tied together heaven and earth. It was the all-inclusive image of the totality of the universe. In the ritual act of ascending the altar (and edifice), the priests acted out the stages of 'god-realization,' and the inner meaning of man's oneness with the cosmos. The Babylonian monarch himself was the focus of the occult power channelled through the activities of the priesthood. He was regarded as a divine being, a god-man. And it was he who contained and maintained the cosmic order on behalf of those he ruled. The monarch's distinctive royal function was to integrate in his own being the powers that govern the universe and his society.

In all respects the esoteric core of the Babylonian gnosis was substantially identical to what we now encounter through Eastern and occult mysticism. The chief distinction is that in those days it was more strictly distributed. In our own times, the seal of secrecy has been broken, and "Mystery Babylon" is spread abroad.

In the highest moment of serene ecstacy the initiate, properly speaking, does not find God. Rather, the mystery of his own being supremely asserts itself. At the end, the only thing that appears to exist (in his universe) is the human self-consciousness moving in sovereign solitude over the void abyss of void existence.

This occult illumination is precisely the opposite of a God-centered orientation to reality. It is radically man-centered and thus it becomes the perfected expression of the Great Lie ("you will be as God") through the logical necessity of its own false presuppositions.[2]

Brooks and I agree that the Bible shows that knowledge, power, and wisdom exist in this other spiritual system, but the system is not according to God. It is based on the lie of the "divine within," and it gets its power from another source. Ezekiel, as God's mouthpiece, points to Babylon and says,

DEATH IN BABYLON

"Your heart is proud, and you have said, 'I am a god, I sit in the seat of the gods . . .' yet you are but a man, and no god" (Ezek. 28:2, RSV).

When Cyrus the Mede crushed Babylon, its secret religion did not disappear from the face of the earth; rather, the whole body of beliefs moved in a variety of directions. Its gods, bearing slightly different names, but in their identity remaining the same, moved to other cultures. Not only did the gods migrate, but across the centuries the very depth of the mystery religion continued to expand. Far from being extinguished, it grew in the very botanical tank of India, where the full genius of the deception would come into bloom, only to blow the spores back across to the Western world. But Babylon of old had the antitypes of the original avatars, celestial beings, mediums, meditators, astrologers, and psychics from whence originated the doctrine of reincarnation in India today. Nimrod, the founder of Babylon, claimed that he would reincarnate as the avatar Tammuz.

Let us now examine the historical record of the migration of some of the Babylonian gods and goddesses to India, not merely the idols of the gods, but their cosmic personalities. These beings, according to the statements of the Apostle Paul, come from the celestial hierarchies of demonic hosts. They are not cultural interest items, or simply Jungian archetypes in the collective unconscious of man, but, in fact, ancient spirit personalities who have tried to mold history across the ages. In the Indian culture, they have been identified more than once as beings of light.

> The Babylonians, in their popular religion, supremely worshipped a goddess mother and son [Semiramis and Tammuz]. From Babylon, this worship of the mother and child spread to the ends of the earth. In Egypt, the mother and child were worshipped under the names of Isis and Osiris. In India, *even to this day*, as Isi and Ishwara. . . .
>
> In Babylon, the title of the goddess-mother as the "dwelling place of God," was Sacca, or in the emphatic form, Sacta, that is, "the tabernacle." Hence, *at this day*,

the great goddess in India, wielding all the power of the god whom she represents, is called "Shakti" or "the tabernacle." [Shakti, as is commonly known, is the female counterpart of the great god Siva.]

It was an essential principle of the Babylonian system, that the sun or Baal was the one only god. When, therefore, Tammuz was worshipped as God incarnate, that implied also that he was an incarnation of the sun. In the *Hindu mythology, which is admitted to* be essentially Babylonian, this comes out very distinctly. There, Surya, or sun, is represented as being incarnate, and born for the purpose of subduing the enemies of the gods, who, without such a birth, could not have been subdued. [There is equally as conclusive evidence regarding the origins of Krishna, Rama, Vishnu, Brahma, Matraiya's Dagon, and a host of other gods and goddesses.][3]

To the pilgrims, the common folk whom we viewed earlier as they swarmed Rishikesh, these gods and goddesses are celestial beings commuting forever from death planes and paradise worlds to the earth. They are cosmic personalities, known to mediumistically possess their worshipers. One of the highest boons of the *sankirtan* ("chanting and singing the names of gods and goddesses for extremely long periods") is that the deity begins to manifest itself through the devotees. Even the great yogis report this phenomenon during the course of their spiritual growth. Ramakrishna was observed by his devotees becoming possessed by Lakshmi, Kali, and Vishnu at various times.

On the higher levels of Hindu *advaitist* ("monistic, or nondualist") philosophy, the kernel of the mystery religion unfolds progressively as the significance of the gods and goddesses is explained. The god or goddess now becomes a cosmic essence or quality, a handle in the realm of maya which the mystic can use to vault into the godhead, the nondual impersonal ocean of Brahman. In short, it is the secret doorway enabling temporal man to become God. Thus, through the eyes of the advanced mystic, the gods and goddesses of the pantheon represent personalizations of abstract higher reality; yet they supposedly have consciousness and can embody persons. Allegedly, they appear before the aspirant for the sake of taking him to the void. Then the gods and goddesses, like the realized mystic, merge back into the indissoluble ocean of Brahman, from whence they never really left but only appeared to leave.

The gods and goddesses become the chrysalis through which the mystic passes in becoming deity. In the case of Ramakrishna, he adored Kali. As a mere human ego, at one point he considered it blasphemy to identify himself as one with Kali. But in time the goddess took him over so much that he found full identification with her. At that point the guru of Ramakrishna told him to shatter her asunder by breaking her image in himself on a shard of glass. He did, and so he was no longer Kali. Instead, he supposedly became "the eternal one," reaching *samadhi* or enlightenment in the process. He went from the dual plane of our ephemeral universe, with its gods and goddesses, to the unborn, "one without a second." Ramakrishna is the prototype success story in our presently emerging mystery religion.

Now we begin to understand that in the mystery religion the gods and goddesses are only intermediates between man and the ultimate God-self. They stand at the gates of death—ego death, physical death, and death to our universe—and beckon the worshiper and mystic through. It is precisely this function that we see among the gods and goddesses and cosmic beings in *The Tibetan Book of the Dead*, so highly praised by Moody. They are the beings of light. The same beings of light fill the accounts of yogis in India and Roshis in Tibet, as we see in our modern accounts. It is a one-for-one correspondence. A being of light is a being of light. If a yogi (as opposed to an American in a hospital) experiences one, and experience is our measuring rod, do we dare deny that there is any difference?

The most famous occult-power *Siddha* yogi ("one who has attained perfection in occult powers") alive in India today, Muktananda, had an experience with a being of light just before he became "enlightened." Let us examine it to see how the experiences of modern yogis relate to Moody's discovery.

> As I again sat for meditation, I felt there was a great commotion around. My entire body started aching and automatically assumed *padmasana*, the lotus posture . . . I felt severe pain in the knot [manipur chakra] below the navel. I tried to shout but could not even articulate. . . . Next I saw ugly and dreadful demon-like figures. I thought them to be evil spirits.
>
> I then saw blazes of fire on all sides and felt that I too was burning. After a while I felt a little better. Suddenly I saw a *large ball of light* approaching me from the front; as it approached, its light grew brighter and brighter. It then entered unobstructed through the closed doors of my *kutir* ["hut"] and merged into my head. My eyes were forcibly closed and I felt a fainting sensation. I was terrified by the powerfully dazzling light.[4]

What we see between the Babylonian gods and goddesses, the Indian gods and goddesses, the modern American reports of premortem beings of light, and the encounters with beings of light by Indian yogis is that they are all one and the same thing. This is a key building block, supplied by the scientific method, that forms the graft to wed the mystical system of Babylon and the mystical system of India with the increasing trend of cosmic humanism on the world scene.

Not only does Moody's being of light tie in with the Eastern system, but so does Kubler-Ross's view of who man really is, his true self. In the concluding chapter of her book *Death: The Final Stage of Growth,* her beliefs emerge. Kubler-Ross chose to entitle the chapter "Omega," the well-known symbol for eternity in the Bible. Christ says, "I am the Alpha and the Omega," three times in the Book of Revelation. I will quote Kubler-Ross liberally to solidify what I hope has become an obvious point. Ask yourself whether this is the biblical definition or the Eastern mystical definition of who man really is.

"There is no need to be afraid of death . . . death is the key to the door of life. . . . It is essential that you become aware of the light, power, and strength within each of you, and that you learn to use those *inner* resources in the service of your own and others' growth. . . . Through commitment to *personal growth* individual human beings will also make their contributions to the growth and development—the evolution—of the whole species to become all that humankind can and is meant to be. *Death is the key to that evolution. . . . The answer is within you.* You can become a *channel* and a source of great inner strength. But you must give up everything in order to gain everything. . . . When human beings 'find a place of stillness and quiet at the highest level of which they are capable, then *the heavenly influences can pour into them,* re-create them, and use *them* for the *Salvation* of mankind.' [Kubler-Ross quotes *The Quiet Mind*]. . . There is no total death. Only the body dies. The *Self* or spirit, or whatever you wish to label it, is eternal. You may interpret this in any way that makes you feel comfortable. . . . You may be more comfortable and comforted by a faith that there is a source of goodness, light, and strength greater than any of us individually, yet still *within us all*, and that each *essential self* has an existence that *transcends* the finiteness of the physical and *contributes to that greater power*. . . . Death, in this context, may be viewed as the curtain between the existence that we are conscious of and the one that is hidden from us until we raise that curtain. . . . It is our purpose as human beings to grow—to *look within ourselves* to find and build upon that source of peace and understanding and strength which *is our inner selves,* and to reach out to others with love, acceptance, patient guidance, and hope for what we all may become together."[5]

The message is clear: the true self transcends death because within it is the source of transcendent existence. The seeds of perfection are within; salvation is from within. The self is eternal and self-sufficient, and within the self is the key, the guide, and the answer for self-evolution. This is the identical definition that Vedantins, yogis, and other forms of Hindus use for "the true self" or *atma*. The Hindu teaching is that the "Atma evolves to Paramatma," which means "the self becomes God." It is a far cry from the biblical account of a fallen and bankrupt soul, incapable of saving itself, whose only salvation is in Christ. Christ told the people that they did not have it within themselves to save themselves.

Indeed, these words of Kubler-Ross could be direct quotes from any number of famous mystics and yogis; the same phrases can be lifted from their writings, whether they be Aurobindo, Ramakrishna, Yogananda, Meher Baba, Madam Blavatsky, or Sat Prem. One wonders what her source of inspiration really was.

As mentioned earlier, Kubler-Ross has a spirit guide, Salem, which by biblical standards makes her a medium.

Consider the following description of Kubler-Ross, and forget the sweet reassurance of her words:

> Then, visibly moved and emanating a glow of awe and wonder, she [Kubler-Ross] shared with us a profound mystical experience that had happened to her only the night before in the midst of a group of seventy-five people. She prefaced her narrative with the remark that only a short time ago she would not have found it possible to speak these words at a public forum. "Last night I was visited by *Salem*, my spirit guide, and two of his companions, Anka and Willie. They were with us until three o'clock in the morning. We talked, laughed and sang together. They spoke and touched me with the most incredible love and tenderness imaginable. This was the highlight of my life."[6]

If we are honest with ourselves about wanting to know the truth, and the Bible speaks about this matter of familiar spirits and spirit guides, we are blinded and liars if we do not consider what it says. It does not compromise.

> And when they say to you, "Consult the mediums and the wizards who whisper and mutter," should not a people consult their God? Should they consult the dead on behalf of the living? (Isa. 8:19, NASB).

We find that at the time of the Babylonian mystery religion, the occult threat of the depraved practices of the Canaanites was so great, its intermixing with God's truth so abhorrent, that God warned about it severely:

Do not turn to mediums and wizards; do not seek them out, to be defiled by them: I am the Lord your God (Lev. 19:31, RSV).

If a person turns to mediums and wizards, playing the harlot after them, I will set my face against that person, and will cut him off from among his people (Lev. 20:6, RSV).

A man or a woman who is a medium or wizard shall be put to death; they shall be stoned with stones, their blood shall be upon them (Lev. 20:27, RSV).

The Bible leaves us with no neutral category in which to put Kubler-Ross. A medium is not an "OK thing." You may say it is harmless, but how do you really know? How many millions of years, tangibly, have you existed in full consciousness without interruption to make a judgment on your own authority? This excludes reincarnation. If you said, "ten million years," I would have to say that those years are a fleeting second compared to the eternity of God, and he says an unequivocal no to fooling with familiar spirits.

To conclude our section on death in the East, what have we found? At the heart of the occult doctrine is the divine-within concept, which was at the center of Babylon's mystery religion, with its concomitant occult arts. This mystery religion, an abomination to the God of the Bible, did not disappear when Babylon was destroyed, but instead continued to grow in India and other regions of the East. What we find today is a rapid acceptance of Indian precepts in the Western world. The scientific community is beginning to embrace it. Indeed, this new mysticism promises to unify all of humanity into a one-world brotherhood, but at a price. Its key message is the "evolution of the self to higher consciousness." Its implied reward is the bestowal of godhood on humanity. Consistent with ancient Egypt, Babylon, India, and the mystics of all ages, it views death as no more than a stage, a transition, for no other reason than that if the soul is immortal, as the higher self, then death is ultimately an illusion. Death becomes mankind's greatest friend. So we have come full circle to the promise in the Garden of Eden.

Before we turn to the revelation of God through the Bible to understand what Scripture says about death, which happens to be quite extensive, we need to examine what it was in the West that has moved us and our thinking from Christ to Krishna, from the prophets to the mediums, from monotheism to monism. Where did the doors open, and how new are the new discoveries?

Is science really unbiased? Have our philosophers really figured it all out? And how did we get from reason to mysticism? In all of this, what have we done with death in the West?

SECTION FOUR

DEATH IN THE WEST— PHILOSOPHY, SCIENCE, AND COSMIC HUMANISM

Coauthored by Robert Schlagal

NINE
THE PRESENT MOOD

The power of the written word affects history in remarkable ways. Visualize a man scrawling on a sheet of paper in a candle-lit room in some shabby, ignominious part of town in the mid-1800s. He is a man we would pass on the street among the throngs of urchins and ordinary folk and think no great thing of it; we would not look twice. In the silence of his study—should we come zooming in by some timeless TV camera—we would hear the scratching of his pen, and we would see the writ unfolding. Should that writ blow away or fall in some trash can, we would feel that the course of the world, the immense gears of history, could proceed well without it. It would make no difference.

Little would we realize that the writ would telescope across half a century to begin an event as titanic as any in modern history. It would create a power bloc encompassing almost half the earth, including the Soviet Union, that sprawling land mass with its Red armies, sophisticated weaponry, and 300 million citizens in ideological enslavement. Russia would churn the world like a mighty dragon about to snap its chains and engulf the world. Yet the power of the writ would extend farther to another land mass, Red China, and add another billion people to the sum.

The writ was *The Communist Manifesto*. The man was Karl Marx. To this day that potent writ continues to shake the world's events, which shows how one body of ideas can affect the course of history. In fact, it has been ideas all along, behind the events of history, which have dethroned one age and thrust up another, including all of the Western world. Far from being an innocuous ivory-tower pastime, philosophy has changed civilizations in the most concrete ways. Marx borrowed from Hegel and Feuerback, and so on, back through history. Most citizens of a specific age cannot articulate the spirit of that age, but it stirs in their thoughts and within them.

The thoughts written on a philosopher's table in one century can rule another century. The question is, How do we fare today in America? From what philosopher's table, or tables, has our culture come? We ask this in the full light of Christianity's fate, for the revelation of man has usurped the revelation of God in the West. We have chosen to believe the supreme wisdom of the philosopher's stone. What kind of world have we inherited? What is our present mood?

A recent Sunday magazine reported that suicides among the nation's adolescents have tripled in the past year.[1] Suicide now outranks any other cause of death, including automobile accidents, among teenagers. Suicide among adults is not far behind.

Two views of death are gaining prominence in today's world. Perhaps these suicides are related to them. One view says there is no afterlife in a godless universe based on pure random creation. Life has no meaning, and therefore death has no significance. The seeds of this view go all the way back to the German rationalists and the British empiricists (who began to throw God out of the equation) and find mature expression in the existentialists of the twentieth century. The other view feels that death is a mystical leap into a happier hereafter. There really is no logic to tie this in; it is just pure belief, groundless faith. If our age, as many have termed it, has become the age of anxiety, or despair, it is predictable that many would begin to look to suicide as either oblivion, hence escape, or a better hereafter, hence escape. Death becomes a release.

The present scientific view of the universe leaves no room for love, for love is an inexplicable oddity, almost an embarrassment. Man is told that love may well be a luxury that he can no longer count on, for present belief leaves a diminishing place for it. The deep assurance of the soul, which Christianity provided when its world view reigned, has been erased. Now only questions and speculations remain, and many of the speculations are hopeless.

Campus moods are either grim or hedonistic. The cynical aside has become the common currency of the day, while few public figures draw genuine respect. Sex roles are turning upside down, and marriage as an institution is on the brink of collapse. People are suspicious of each other and wonder who, if any, is truly good. Is goodness possible? it is asked. Everyone seems to be "in it for himself." In the scientific community the idea of finding meaning to life has all but been abandoned as a romantic and antiquated notion that suited a bygone era. Daily newspapers reinforce our cynicism that man cannot be rehabilitated after all, that "the Great Society" is a lie, that it is all "going down the tube." Random senseless killings tell us this, especially when the killer gets off scot-free. We see Son of Sam smiling on the cover of *Newsweek* and we groan.

Scores of scientific authorities openly contradict one another as they offer solutions to the world's problems. Meanwhile, the landscape of civilization groans like a giant beast. The skyline is ugly, for in place of the natural wilderness that was once America, raw pollution oozes out as the fecal matter of sprawling civilization. Environmentalists examine air and water and proclaim the ecological crisis. Everything that man touches seems to turn to sludge.

But death is also a threat in an atmosphere of negativity. We either shut it out of our minds and cellophane wrap our coffins, or we dispose of death with nervous quips of black humor. Our lives go at such a furious pace that we do not allow the thought of death to creep in, while solitude is avoided at all costs, in the event that we might become morbid. Then come all the escapes: liquor, TV, sex, drugs, hobbies, work, sports, and anything else that will get in the way and shut out the growing vacuum. Yet many of the escapes are no longer working, now that it is possible to be lonely even in a crowd of friends. Man seems to be reaching a dead end, the self-fulfilling prophecy of Sartre's *No Exit*.

As a child of our age, I was only too familiar with the contemporary malaise. Cynicism was epidemic at every high school I attended. To echo Bob Dylan's words, it seemed that "not much was really very sacred." The ideals so exalted in the "old days" were gutted with the glibness of TV talk shows, as we questioned if there was any enduring value to love, marriage, life, God, or anything else. To be sure, we were not oblivious to the fact that such things were crumbling about us in a stock market crash of values that plummeted as doubts increased. "What is worth living for?" we asked. This was the dilemma that caused so many of us to act in rage. We were a generation that protested in disillusionment, rioted, marched, jibed, and got into trouble constantly.

But on a deeper level, such antisocial acts were simply the ghosts of the previous generations' beliefs about life coming back to haunt them in full-blooded imagery. The kids provided the embarrassing afterthoughts. After all, how can death be a sacred institution in an age of relativism? Who or what deserves respect in a universe with man at the top? There are no ideals. Nor is there freedom or dignity in a Skinnerian behavioristic world.

We were reacting with a gut response, not realizing that we lived in a post-Christian world. University scientists and grammer-school textbooks, as well as the school books in between, clearly gave us the message that there was no personal God, only the hope of man saving himself. And it was not altogether clear, either, who man was. Desmond Morris told us he was a "naked ape." Monod, a geneticist, told us man was an accident, and Camus and Sartre told us he was a joke. A contemporary cartoon summed it all up by picturing a child standing before a group while "decked out" in flippers, ballet dress, football helmet, catcher's mask, Donald Duck beak, hockey kneepads, with a baseball bat in one hand and a baton in the other. Identity was no longer clear, coherent, or stable.

The philosophy of science left us with such a bleak picture that there was only one other option (if one was no longer willing to consider revealed religion): mysticism. That door has been hurled open with almost violent force. Many threw out cold logic with utter disdain and jumped into the "higher gear" of nonrational intuition.

The Beatles, Timothy Leary, psychedelia, the occult, and the Eastern gurus flooded in with cataclysmic force, creating an intoxicating optimism. Haight-Ashbury sang about flower power, and a new generation of young, mystically oriented scientists was on the way. They were from our generation, youth of the sixties, who were fed up with rationalistic presuppositions. Instead, these scientists would try to make the facts of science fit a new paradigm and harmonize with the view that everything is evolving into pure consciousness. Today, Carl Sagan smiles on the cover of *Newsweek*, assuring us that we are not alone in the universe. Books like *The Tao of Physics* proliferate, while anthropologist Castaneda tells us of his mystical findings. The bridge for the new thanatology has been laid.

Death research would close the gap between present knowledge and the mystical view of afterlife. The new faith of death would then triumphantly demolish the bankruptcy of despair, which has been so much the spirit of the modern age. People would grab onto it with a greedy bias. Even reason might be discarded in the scramble. This is how Moody and Kubler-Ross found such a timely niche in the historical progression of our age. What modern man now has is the view of death examined in chapter one, "Sudden Death."

Sam Jones or Fred Smith can abandon humanist despair for a groundless hope wherein each can hunger for the day when the gentle doorway of death eases him into a blissful love-filled hereafter. What a balm to replace a cruel and impersonal world. Yet biblically, this is the sweetest lie of all.

To see more clearly how we got where we are in the West, we will peer back to some key moments in recent history. We must do this to be honest in our search.[2] Then the spirit of the age will reveal itself.

TEN
THE DEATH
OF GOD

The occult epidemic has hit the West. In ten years it has become a best-selling enterprise. The view of death propagated by Moody and Kubler-Ross is directly linked to the teachings of the mystical occult tradition. Why is such a growing number of scientific investigators and the general public so receptive to this vision? Why now? How did we leap from scientific naturalism to nonrational mysticism in the midst of such a skeptical "scientific age"? How was the old view of the supernatural disposed of to bring in this new view of the supernatural?

In this century we have seen the secular naturalistic view replace the Christian faith and its statements about reality, God, and the universe. This is the philosophy of science. Naturalism asserts that the natural phenomena of the universe are its exhaustive reality and that life has no divine, supernatural source or meaning. This has created a great vacuum. So in the midst of the vaunted enlightenment of the twentieth century, all types of occult spiritualism have flooded in because Kant and Hegel jammed a stick of dynamite into the philosophical presuppositions which heralded the Age of Reason. They asked the empiricists, "How do you know that you know?" In a trice, knowledge was limited to a miniscule area within "pure reason." But it would take science several centuries to realize the blow on the head that it had received then.

What had not dawned on anyone was that a giant gulf had been created between the rational objective realm of scientifically observable facts and everything invisible that has value for us (love, truth, right, wrong, good, evil, God). Man, a combination of the material and spiritual, was divided right down the middle by the Kant-Hegel system and made an amputee. He could only have inner feelings as to what was right and wrong; he could never really know. Kierkegaard soon came along and put on the finishing touches to the gulf to make the barrier between the physical and the spiritual totally impassable. Faith, he said, could have no relation whatsoever to the physical, the rational, the concrete. Faith was a blind leap into the unknown. As Schaeffer and Rushdoony suggest, this brought about modern existentialism and modern despair. A mystic, a saint, and a schizophrenic were now in the same ball park. Choose your "trip" and don't worry about proving it, because you can't anyway.

An Orientalist, Lucien Styrk, remarks in his anthology of Buddhistic literature, *The World of the Buddha*, that the popularity of Buddhism in the West results, "not because other systems of belief have failed in their purpose but because, simply, they have been unable to coexist with those views of reality offered by science and humanistic disciplines." Man has become the judge of reality from within outward; this is humanism. Humanism is man-centered. The occult is man-centered. Christianity is not man-centered; it is God-centered.

Disposing of Christianity several hundred years ago, a number of philosophers defined what acceptable knowledge was: the "known" was observable phenomena, the method was the empirical method, and by definition it had (a priori) to shut out anything that was not in this category. That was their criterion for truth, and it excluded the God of the Bible. These men were the British empiricists (Locke, Berkeley, and Hume) and the continental rationalists (Descartes, Leibnitz, and Spinoza). They had their differences, but it was like an in-family battle (see the Appendixes for clarification).

Skeptical empiricism, with its anti-Christian bias, has become the dominant mode for understanding reality in the West. Its assumptions go unquestioned, and its voice has become almost a religious oracle for us as it strays out of its field into other areas.

Yet, by accurate definition, any concern with the invisible—religion, ethical values, metaphysics—is not within the province of science, whose business extends no further than the observation and collation of data. Speculations and statements about ultimate reality and meanings behind the universe are not proper to science, because science studies observable and repeatable phenomena piecemeal and from the outside. That study cannot discover the power and purpose behind reality. As C. S. Lewis remarked in *Mere Christianity*, "If there was a controlling power outside the universe, it would not show itself to us as one of the facts inside the universe—no more than the architect of a house could actually be a wall or staircase or fireplace in that house."[1]

All the same, the language of science has become synonymous with the language of truth. The result is that the description of anything in scientific jargon (with apparent scientific detachment) creates an overwhelming impression of authority and authenticity. A case in point, as was mentioned earlier, is the format in which Moody presents his "data." Science is speaking here in the province of religion, and his scientific language consoles us with a religious belief in life after death (with none of the unpleasantness or demands of a biblical God, before whom men are morally accountable). People are grabbing onto it like a life raft in a pitching storm, because the other alternative, that they have been faced with so long, is despair. All men wish to feel that life is something more than brute chance, and death more than total annihilation. Indeed, whenever a society is permeated by the deep uncertainties which now possess ours, men tend to oscillate between deep skepticism and cynicism on the one hand and mysticism on the other.

Our spiritual crisis in the West has its roots in the Age of Reason, that eighteenth-century period out of which emerged the rationalists and the empiricists. In this age, strains of humanistic, man-centered thought came together and flourished, producing a widespread change in assumptions about reality. It was a revolutionary age that introduced the ideas which have become the basis of our modern thought. The working out of these assumptions over the last three hundred years has brought us into T. S. Eliot's "wasteland."

The Age of Reason taught that the mind of man was an all-sufficient, autonomous agent for comprehensively understanding human nature and reality. Yet we forget that only a small percentage of thinkers brought us into the Age of Reason. This minority asserted that human intelligence could comprehend man and the world with adequacy. But the facts of life seem to tell us otherwise; the frightening brevity of life, the vastness of the world, and the limited experience of man, given his small allotment of time and space, should tell us that man is going beyond himself in so ambitious a project as to try to logically disassemble, and account for, the cosmos. The task requires an overview that is more than humanly derived. If there is a purpose behind the universe, it is too vast for us to discover or conceive; it seems like an ant trying to comprehend a Mahler symphony. The only alternative in so staggering a project is for a mind greater than the cosmos to reveal its true purpose to us; an intelligence any less in magnitude is not equipped to give us an ultimate answer.

In the Age of Reason the transcendental supernatural basis for existence was thrown out. If by definition God could not speak, the only alternative was for man to turn his faith toward himself as the final judge of truth. If man could not have access to God by his reason or physical experience, then God was at root unknowable, if not nonexistent. That is quite an assumption.

To prove that God was a myth, the irreverent Voltaire proudly averred, "If God did not exist, it would be necessary to invent him." All things knowable, the Age of Reason insisted, had to begin with man and his mind and experience. Any fact that could not meet this standard was tossed out as superstition. The only facts that could have reality were those to which science had access; thus, science came to the prejudiced assertion that "whatever my net does not catch is not fish." Much is too large and much is too small to fit the net.

Subtly, science was transformed from a method to a faith. It went from a simple method of observation to an entire perspective about reality, which in itself was taken on faith (this is called "scientism"). At a sweep, man's most meaningful perception of himself as a mind, body, and soul created with purpose by an infinite God was denied and brushed aside. The Bible was defunct.

As the Age of Reason made pronouncements about the validity or invalidity of various approaches to knowledge, the arena of philosophic inquiry shifted from ontology, the study of the nature of being and reality, to epistemology, the theory of knowledge. This means that the concern of thinkers shifted from the study of God and God's universe to the study of the human mind and its limitations. As Kant had asked, "What can the mind know, how does it know, and how does it know that it knows?" The modern thinkers have continued to ask this same question since the time of Kant. Man as opposed to God was advanced as the central and definitive fact in the universe. Man could touch and feel himself, and that was all that was needed to prove to most men that they existed, though some philosophers quibbled over this as well.

But by killing God, man was also murdering himself and his own significance. As a consequence, today many men can echo Jean Paul Sartre when he concludes that "man is a meaningless passion." If what the rationalists and empiricists were saying is true, then man's significance lies in his being a part of the natural world, in relationship to scientifically discerned facts. Without God, in whose image man has been made, man is no more than a fact among facts, an animal among animals, and he is no more significant than a fragment of quartz or an amoeba. Today man is not even the man he was yesterday. Even his definition changes day by day. Man has recently become a sociophysical behavior configuration which ought to be studied in the same way that the behavior of chemical compounds is studied.

Where is man's real identity? The human face has all but disappeared from modern painting and sculpture; when it does appear, it is either an element in design or something nonhuman that is worthy of contempt, disgust, or horror. As a result of man's loss of God-guaranteed identity, man has become something without a soul which can be molded like putty into any shape desired by a government bureaucrat, psychologist, social engineer, or educator. Man tries to become God and in the process destroys himself.

This is precisely the terrible vision that George Orwell had when he wrote 1984 in the forties— of man taking on the responsibility of playing God and creating a nightmare. Doubtless the Nazi concentration camps were not far from Orwell's mind. If anything, history shows that man makes a cruel and insane god; every Caesar and every dictator proves this point.

But what was the Christian view before the rationalists threw it out? Man at that time knew himself as a fallen creature within a fallen universe, and both were utterly dependent upon the grace of God for stability, continuity, and comprehensibility. All of man's experience in this life was intelligible through faith in God's self-revelation in history. Life and death, good and evil, and suffering and grief were not lost in the dark, impenetrable mystery of chance and blind evolution. They were comprehended through the sovereign plan of God across the ages. In the Judeo-Christian universe, certain things were given philosophically: through God we know that we live in a world of his creation which is rational and purposive. Though we do not possess the minds to comprehend it fully, we know that our minds are suited to understanding the universe in limited ways. We know that the material universe is objective and real, that time and space and causality are not illusions but part of the actual form and structure of this universe. We know that we are each known and loved individually by God and that our personalities are real and significant. We also realize that we are morally accountable before this God and that our life actions are not random and meaningless, but significant enough to one day receive judgment.

It is now understandable, therefore, that when the Age of Reason uprooted this foundation, a crisis ensued. The model of the universe that man had cherished was no longer assured, but it would take time for the import of this to fully dawn upon man. Some say it has taken three centuries. In a sense, the Age of Reason was "the great revolt." When a ship full of ignorant and rebellious slaves mutiny in mid sea and kill the captain and his officers, they may be able to operate the ship. But if they are unable to read the charts and steer the ship, their successful rebellion becomes their own defeat, for eventually they will be lost, wrecked, and marooned. Was this what happened to rationalism with its heady ambitions? Did it give us its promised utopia? The promise is still there, looming in the air like a supermart special. Science still says, "Just wait, the answer is just around the corner," but its voice is quickly losing the authority it once had.

Perhaps the problem is most clearly summed up by that brilliant insightful journalist, the former editor of *Punch*, Malcolm Muggeridge:

> It is difficult to resist the conclusion that there is a death wish at work at the heart of our civilization whereby our banks promote the inflation which will ruin them, our educationalists seem to create the moral and intellectual chaos which will nullify their professional purposes, our physicians invent new and more terrible diseases to replace those they have abolished, our moralists cut away the roots of all morality and our theologians dismantle the structure of belief they exist to expound and promote.[2]

After years of scathing cynicism and learning, and after years of acute observation, Muggeridge became a Christian. He says his conversion was not at all a copout; it was a most sane and rational conclusion, and it changed him from the inside out. To this day, Christianity links the world of the rational to the spiritual. It shows the harmony and continuity of all knowledge. It works. Not a scientist is alive who can look out to the distant galaxies and quasars, which are millions of light years away, and then look at the teeming microbes beneath his feet and explain how they got there. The scientists do not know; they are still theorizing. Their best attempt so far at an explanation is that it is all somehow a kind of an accident, which is a paltry response to an immense question.

The domain of science has been the observable, the rational. All that the secular philosophy of science has done has left us with a headful of questions and a spiritual identity crisis in our souls. Personal experience alone tells us that we are more than just chemicals. How could the scientistic philosophy fully satisfy our needs if there is a whole spiritual side to our nature? It does not matter whether science recognizes this or not; it is there. Through the lens of science we have played a charade, pretending to be what we are not; like the proverbial mental patient, we can freeze in the garden and pretend to be cornstalks, but after enough rain and cold, and after we have missed a few meals, we will soon become fidgety and even more clearly betray our real nature. We are not cornstalks any more than we are just chemicals.

But such an answer cannot satisfy for long. A wide shift has begun among the public. Many are leaving science's domain of the rational and turning to that other alternative, the extrarational, the intuitive, the spiritual, the occult. Keep in mind that they have inherited the belief (from Kant, Hegel, and Kierkegaard) that there will never be a unified field of knowledge encompassing the physical universe with any spiritual reality, should one even exist. They are being forced to take a leap of faith, as Kierkegaard provided, and the only judges they know of are their own inner senses. The peril, of course, is that a sheep will follow its leader right to a cliff's edge and jump over. In an unchartered nonrational void, there is a similarity between the sheep and the seeker.

People now gear their lives by truly unprovable things. Syndicated astrology columns appear daily in nearly every newspaper in the country; if people were not interested, they would not be there. Transcendental meditation has become a multinational corporation. A growing din of spiritual voices fills the air, and every brand of teacher is available. This is exactly what the Bible predicted would happen: "False Christs and false prophets will arise and show great signs and wonders, so as to lead astray, if possible, even the elect" (Matt. 24:24, RSV). It seems that the stage is being set for a large-scale mystery religion. The problem is, once people have been persuaded (or seduced) into abandoning reason, you cannot reason with them. The concrete result is the physicist who "throws the *I Ching*," the occult Chinese book of fortune, and the pragmatist who is willing to be guided by the invisible. It is a little reminiscent of Kubler-Ross being guided by Salem.

In conclusion, the West has regressed to the forbidden land of occultic "superstition," which its enlightened enterprise of rationalism promised to abolish. In the eighteenth century, the West assumed the posture of mature humanity in an Age of Reason now sufficiently civilized to leave behind the "superstitions" which had so "limited its potential." Overnight, God was labeled as an obsolete "concept" not relevant to the new definition of acceptable knowledge. Man proudly assumed he could create a unified field of knowledge which could contain as well as explain reality and existence. Rational man was exalted. Knowing all things, man could become godlike. He could begin to assume control over increasing domains and perfect his world.

But it did not work. No unified body of knowledge has emerged that can honestly answer all of man's deepest questions. Literature and the arts do not speak of a utopian world, but spew out bitter, nihilistic, and angry messages about the state of man. Man today feels more like a bag of chemicals, a piece of merchandise, than a god. He has lost his spiritual estate, and society has become impersonal, cold, and repressive.

If there is some kind of cosmic malignant intelligence, as the Bible states, then the magic trick took place when modern man leaped from the checkmated position of rationalist despair to the extrarational free fall of blind faith. Without any spiritual guidelines, man is now truly vulnerable in a wholly new way. He has returned to a primitive inner-directed religious subjectivism—from spiritualism, to pantheism, and even devil worship. Truly, this equation begins to look more and more like some diabolical tour de force.

The only final alternative left in our wide search is the transcendent, personal God of the universe, who ordained all order and at times intervened in history to provide us with knowledge and revelation, which we in our own efforts could never uncover. This is the ultimate Author of the Bible and the sovereign Creator.

SECTION FIVE

THE REVELATION OF GOD

ELEVEN
THE ETERNAL WORD

The grass withers, the flower fades; but the word of our God shall stand for ever (Isa. 40:8, Revised Berkeley).

The Bible stands at the apex of all books ever written in history. There are enough amazing facts about it to fill a *Guiness Book of World Records*, yet few people are aware of them, and few have bothered to do more than flip through the Bible once or twice in a lifetime. For most people, the Bible is merely a book filling a space in a bookcase collecting dust. They have a smooth array of pat answers which they can summon up when questioned about the Bible, but the truth is that public ignorance about the Bible is staggering. We will survey a few of the remarkable facts about the Bible before quoting it, for to quote the Bible without the amazing perspective behind it is to do it and ourselves a great injustice. We need to realize that the Bible itself is a miracle, and that the history alone of this supernatural book pales any other historical drama. The Bible refers to itself as the Word of God, unlike any other book in existence.

Let us try to view the Bible from God's point of view to see why such a revelation should be given to the human race. Above such questions as Did Christ live? Are there miracles? and Has the Bible prophesied the future again and again from one age to another? is an even more basic question: Is the

Bible's ultimate author God and not the amazingly harmonious lineage of prophets and scribes who did the actual speaking and recording? Have God's communications been coming through clearly? Or, to look at the problem from another angle, If there really is a God who created the universe, then is it not within his power to actually enter history and reveal himself? And would he not do so if his creation of man had a purpose after all, and was not some random event? If man had purpose, then God would be negligent if man were left alone to grope in the dark and puzzle things out for himself, especially if it were beyond man's capacities to arrive at ultimate solutions.

From our human perspective, we could say that the complex creation around man plus his abilities seem to testify to the fact that man has significance. He is more than just a bag of chemicals. Rather, if man's intelligence, will, and emotions are more than haphazard results of creation, then they really do have a purpose. Man, through all of his faculties, can receive and understand communications about the meaning and purpose of the whys and wherefores of existence itself. God could and would reach from the infinite down to the finite, cross the gulf that man could never cross, and directly intervene in our world.

This is exactly what the Bible claims has happened. God intervened in history, and the Bible is the record of that intervention. Man did not just perform some religious rite and summon so great a One as God into speaking. Rather, God himself purposed his communications in his own way and on his own terms, which has always been a problem to many.

God chose people of incredible integrity through whom he would give his Word. His prophets were utterly different from the mediums and psychics of Babylon and the East, both in simple, humble, human character, and in morals. Rather than receiving subjective inner experiences, his prophets had the inner quickening of the fire of the Holy Spirit; they were enlivened with active and not passive minds. They felt the awesome power of their living God, and they were 100 percent accurate in what they said and predicted, with miracles occurring time and time again to support their words. Above all, they testified that their revelations were from a transcendent, holy God, before whom all they could do was to fall upon their faces. They never even hinted at a divine-within experience or a higher-self experience.

Why the need for revelation? Because even if man had a billion years of uninterrupted laboratory investigation, and had broken down all the material and mechanical facts behind the physical universe, he would still be ignorant of the much higher qualities of spiritual reality. He could not squeeze good and evil out of a frozen charge of energy. Man would be approaching the whole problem in an upside-down fashion. Not that there is not a clear continuum tying the physical to the spiritual, but simply, from man's point of view, he lacks the resources to tie them together (as we have seen from the rationalists, then Kant, and Kierkegaard). Something lesser cannot transcend itself to understand the greater. An idiot will never understand cybernetics or James Joyce. And certainly man's billion-year-old laboratory would never go beyond the universe to peer into the character of an infinite God. We must understand this in order to comprehend the need for revelation.

Having seen that need, let us briefly examine the substance of the revelation, the record, and its format. F. F. Bruce, a foremost Bible scholar, defines the range of the Bible:

> The Bible, at first sight, appears to be a collection of literature—mainly Jewish. If we enquire into the circumstances under which the various Biblical documents were written, we find that they were written at intervals over a space of nearly 1400 years. The writers wrote in various lands, from Italy in the west of Mesopotamia and possibly Persia in the east. The writers themselves were a heterogeneous number of people, not only separated from each other by hundreds of years and hundreds of miles, but belonging to the most diverse walks of life. In their ranks we have kings, herdsmen, soldiers, legislators, fishermen, statesmen, courtiers, priests and prophets, a tentmaking Rabbi and a Gentile physician, not to speak of others of whom we know nothing apart from the writings they have left us. The writings themselves belong to a great variety of

literary types. They include history, law (civil, criminal, ethical, ritual, sanitary), religious poetry, didactic treatises, lyric poetry, parable and allegory, biography, personal correspondence, personal memoirs and diaries, in addition to the distinctively Biblical types of prophecy and apocalyptic.

For all that, the Bible is not simply an anthology; there is a unity which binds the whole together. An anthology is compiled by an anthologist, but no anthologist compiled the Bible.[1]

What stands out in all that testifies against merely human authorship is the profound unity of thought in the Bible. Josh McDowell, after citing the above passage in his own book, recounts,

A representative of the Great Books of The Western World came to my house recruiting salesmen for their series. He spread out the chart of the Great Books of The Western World series. He spent five minutes talking to us about . . . the series and we spent an hour and a half talking to him about the Greatest Book.

I challenged him to take just 10 of the authors, all from one walk of life, one generation, one place, one time, one mood, one continent, one language, and just one controversial subject (the Bible speaks on hundreds with harmony and agreement). Then I asked him: "Would they (the authors) agree?" He paused and then replied, "No!" "What would you have?" I retorted. Immediately he said, "A conglomeration." Two days later he committed his life to Christ (the theme of the Bible).[2]

The format alone of the Bible displays incredible unity. The Bible speaks single-mindedly from scores of people, recording historical events as it teaches, which shows that it was tangibly given across time. Is this important? Yes, the Bible's regard for tangible history is an important philosophical comment on the nature of reality. As opposed to the Hindu teaching of maya, which says everything is an illusion, God proclaims his creation to be fully real. And there is more. History offers evidence of real events, which a reasonable

individual would require in making a decision of fai
not a blind leap. Our minds require some kind of
knowledge that biblical events actually occurred
ascertain this?

Consider that in America today we all stand upon a foundation of prior events in history—civilizations have come and gone; wars, eras, fashions, inventions, and great men have preceded us, all of them directly affecting where we are right now. We know that America had a Civil War, for we have all kinds of written records about it, from the memoirs of soldiers and their families to government documents and records in the archives. Also, Civil War ruins, monuments, relics, coins, guns, cannons, maps, and such evidence as the names of streets testify that the war really occurred. That war had an effect on where America is today, and other events that were as real as the Civil War just as tangibly brought about the war and the events that happened prior to it. Those earlier events, such as the American Revolution and the voyage of Columbus, left their marks upon us as well. America did not just spring out of nowhere; it emerged from an historical progression of events, and there is plenty of evidence today that they took place. The same historical argument holds true for Christ's appearance.

Too much evidence of the Christ event exists historically, geographically, and archaeologically to deny it. To deny the evidence would be to deny all of ancient history, including the Roman Empire. Israel is a treasure house, with its documents, Dead Sea Scrolls, Jewish records, ruins, coins, and other numerous items, and historians of that time supply accounts of Christ and his followers. Roman historian Tacitus (born A.D. 53) says that Nero blamed the burning of Rome on the Christians, and that it was Pontius Pilate who put Christ to death; Flavius Josephus, a Jewish historian, mentions numerous miracles of Christ in his famous *Antiquities* (xviii. 33), written early in the second century; and Thallus, another Roman historian, blamed the universally accepted darkening of the sky at Christ's crucifixion on "an eclipse." Meanwhile, Sir William A. Ramsay, the famous archaeologist, referred to the Book of Acts as "an authority for the topography, antiquities, and society of Asia Minor." But the greatest historical sources of the life and times of Christ are detailed in the New Testament.

However, most people dismiss the New Testament records as biased and therefore invalid. But this argument of "bias" is an argument that historiography will not tolerate. An eyewitness account is an eyewitness account; the legal profession stands on this. Because the New Testament is a primary eyewitness document, judicial evidence can be brought to bear on it in legal inquiry. A number of the most brilliant legal minds have sought to use judicial evidence to depose once and for all the New Testament record, especially the resurrection account. One of these men, Simon Greenleaf, was the famous Royall professor of law at the Harvard Law School and succeeded Justice Story as the Dane professor of law. Greenleaf's outstanding contribution to the field of law was a work entitled *A Treatise on the Law of Evidence*, which H. Knott, a legal authority, says "is still considered the single greatest authority on evidence in the entire literature of legal procedure." Greenleaf's conclusion after submitting the New Testament accounts to the most rigorous juridical analyses was that the Gospels had an impenetrable defense that would hold up in any court of law. Greenleaf became a believer. His extensive inquiry is entitled *An Examination of the Testimony of the Four Evangelists by the Rules of Evidence Administered in the Courts of Justice*.[3]

By legal procedure, the New Testament is indisputable. But one might still ask, "Yes, but how are we sure that these biblical documents have not been tampered with over the ages? How do they compare to the originals?"

First, the time gap between the writing of the Gospels and the ascent of Christ was no more than the gap separating us from World War II. So the Gospels were completely contemporary, just as today scores of eyewitnesses are living who saw World War II, and numerous highly detailed accounts have been written about it. In his own day, Peter the apostle said, "For we did not follow cleverly devised tales when we made known to you the power and coming of our Lord Jesus Christ, but we were eyewitnesses of His majesty" (2 Pet. 1:16, NASB). When Peter wrote his accounts, scores of eyewitnesses were alive who could have challenged historical falsehoods and said, "Everybody knows that the Sanhedrin discounted Christ's resurrection. Why, they paraded the corpse through the streets of Jerusalem." But people in the apostle's day could not say this. If the resurrection had been disproven by the authorities of the day, certainly Peter's preaching in Jerusalem itself, only months after the crucifixion, would not have resulted in the conversion of over two thousand Jews in a single afternoon. The common people knew that something incredible was happening. Contradictory evidence would have stopped Christianity and the New Testament documents right then and there. We will examine this closer, since it is a very important point.

The Book of Acts cites that at one point five hundred people saw the resurrected Christ in full view. J. N. D. Anderson, a professor of law, says, "Think of the number of witnesses, over 500. Think of the character of the witnesses, men and women who gave the world the highest ethical teaching it has ever known, and who even on the testimony of enemies lived it out in their lives. Think of the psychological absurdity of picturing a little band of defeated cowards cowering in an upper room one day and a few days later transformed into a company that no persecution could silence—and then attempting to attribute this dramatic change to nothing more convincing than a miserable fabrication they were trying to foist upon the world. That simply would not make sense."[4]

No one will proceed with a willful deception when it involves his life, and hosts of the early Christians were painfully martyred. This makes it clearer why the contemporaries of the New Testament writers did not refute their writings, and how these eyewitness accounts could be written in their day and stand. But we are still left with the question asked earlier: How do today's New Testament records match the original ones?

A. T. Robertson, a manuscript authority, says, "There are some 8,000 manuscripts of the Latin Vulgate and at least 1,000 for the other early versions. Add over 4,000 Greek manuscripts and we have 13,000 manuscript copies of portions of the New Testament. Besides all of this, much of the New Testament can be reproduced from the quotations of the early Christian writers."[5]

Comparing today's best translations with the most ancient records, there are no essential differences. Sir Frederic G. Kenyon, another manuscript authority, states, "The interval then between the dates of the original composition and the earliest extant evidence becomes so small as to be in fact negligible, and the last foundation of any doubt that the scriptures have come down to us substantially as they were written has now been removed. Both the authenticity and the general integrity of the books of the New Testament may be regarded as finally established."[6]

Various copies from over the past seventeen hundred years have had no essential differences! Indeed, the remarkable preservation of the New Testament seems to be exactly as Christ himself predicted, "Heaven and earth will pass away, but My words will not pass away" (Luke 21:33, NASB). Yet should this surprise us when we consider that if God can hold the galaxies in their courses, he can preserve his revelation? The Word of God has remained miraculously intact over the ages; and when one considers some of the attempts throughout history to blot it out, the entire picture becomes even more incredible.

Having seen the Bible's incredible range, that it speaks with a single mind, that history and archaeology support it, that its internal evidence would stand in any court of law, and that the manuscripts have been preserved with incredible accuracy, we must consider another aspect of the Bible, which points even more obviously to its unique distinction of being a miraculous book: prophecy. In hundreds of places, the Bible has foretold events with absolute accuracy, often centuries before they occurred. No other book in the world can claim this. The advent of Christ was prophesied in the Old Testament hundreds of years before his birth. Predictive prophecy further says that a supreme, all-knowing intelligence is behind the Bible.

The most incredible prophecies concern the very cornerstone of the Bible, Jesus Christ. Written in great detail centuries before his birth, they state where and when he would be born; of what lineage; and his purpose, mission, death, and ascent. The staggering fact is that 332 specific Old Testament prophecies are about Christ (see Appendix 3).

Equally incredible is what this means if one considers the exact fulfillment of these prophecies in terms of the science of mathematical probability; they constitute an impossibility if left to blind chance, and a divine miracle if fulfilled, as they have been. Mathematician Peter Stoner reports that the chance of just 48 of the prophecies coming true by accident is 1 in 10^{157}, a number so vast that it is greater than the number of estimated atoms in the entire universe (see Appendix 3). This constitutes a miracle. The common rebuttal, however, is: But how do we know that these prophecies were not written after Christ, and after the fact? The answer is: because the Jews and their Bible-based civilization existed for centuries before Christ. Their entire life structure and orientation were based on the Old Testament laws and prophecies, from the writings of Moses, the psalms of David, and the proverbs of Solomon, to the prophecies of Isaiah and Ezekiel.

How do we know that the Old Testament prophecies preceded Christ? Here is absolute proof: "The Septuagint, the Greek translation of the Hebrew scripture, was completed in the reign of Ptolemy Philadelphus (285-246 B.C.). It is rather obvious that if you have a Greek translation in 250 B.C., then you had to have the Hebrew text from which it was written in 250 B.C. This will suffice to indicate that there was at least a 250-year gap between the prophecies being written down and their fulfillment in the Person of Christ."[7]

What about the corruption of the Old Testament text? Consider this: If a Hebrew scribe in the ancient world miscopied even a single letter on a given day, he would burn that particular parchment, leave the school, bathe in a river, and pray the remainder of the day. Everything he wrote was read and reread for errors by rabbis and overviewers. The result was that when the Dead Sea Scrolls were discovered, they were found to be almost two thousand years old. Obviously they had remained untouched. Previously, the oldest manuscript of Isaiah, known as the Masoretic text, dated back to A.D. 916. The Dead Sea Scrolls are a thousand years older, and the Masoretic text had a thousand extra years of transcription beyond the Dead Sea Scrolls. When the two texts were compared, they were essentially identical. Geisler and Nix state in their general introduction to the Bible that between the two Isaiah scrolls, "in one chapter of 166 words, there is only one word (three letters) in question after a thousand years of transmission—and this word does not significantly change the meaning of the passage." [8] The Old Testament, like the New Testament, has been transmitted essentially without error over the ages.

To get to the heart of the matter, when one sees the immense effort put into a book like the Bible, he can conclude that at the very least it is trying to make a point, and that not to consider its communications would be genuine foolishness. Revealed sufficiently in the Bible's revelations are the character of God, the scheme of creation and ultimate reality, absolute spiritual values, and the coming history of the ages as it is progressively unfolded. As mentioned earlier, at its cornerstone—where all prophecy points—is the advent of Christ, the expression of the written eternal Word as the living Word, the ultimate intervention of God in history. He is the messianic concept of "Emmanuel" or "God with us." As the God-man, Christ is God's final revelation of his own essential nature, a fact large enough for anyone to comprehend. This fact of Christ's deity became the stumbling block of the world, yet Christ is the ultimate bridge between man and the eternal God. No other route, no other alternative, will be given. The great mystery lies in the ransom sacrifice, the final release for many. The crucifixion, as we shall see in chapter 12, is the ultimate release from the power of death. For now, let us look briefly into the mystery of the true identity of Christ, for the Bible is preoccupied with this issue.

In every gospel, in chapter after chapter, Christ is found claiming incredible things for himself, unlike anyone who ever existed. Christ claimed the power to forgive sins, he controlled the forces of nature, he claimed authority over venerable tradition, and he boldly predicted his own resurrection and return to judge the world. As Pinnock says, "Eventually the authorities had enough of it and put Him to death for blasphemy. Jesus was not unwilling to die, for He saw death as part of His redeeming mission, but He reiterated time and again that death would not hold Him, and that His resurrection would decisively prove His claims."[9]

The one nation that would not take a man's claim to deity

lightly was the Jewish nation, which feared and venerated the names of their God (Jehovah, Elohim, etc.). If a man were to try to set himself up and pretend the role, Israel was not the place to do it; Greece, Rome, Egypt, or Persia, perhaps, but not Israel. As he led an utterly sober and blameless life, Christ would describe himself in the identical Old Testament language used for Jehovah alone: "Before Abraham was, I am" (John 8:58); "He who has seen Me has seen the Father" (John 14:9, NASB); and, like Jehovah, he was referred to as the Creator (John 1:3), the Savior, the Judge, the Light of the world, the Glory of God, the Redeemer, the Forgiver of sins, and the Alpha and Omega. All of these are attributed to God in the Old Testament. The Jews knew that only One was deserving of worship, God. And Christ received worship from a leper, from Thomas, and others, and the Epistle to the Hebrews says that even the very angels adored and worshiped Christ (Heb. 1:6), an honor that was out of the question for a mere mortal, a mere created being. When Stephen the martyr was stoned to death, he prayed to Christ to receive his spirit (Acts 7:59).

It seems evident at this point that Christ's claim to deity was very real, and the implications of what this means have never been put better than in the words of C. S. Lewis: "I am trying here to prevent anyone saying the really foolish thing that people often say about Him: 'I'm ready to accept Jesus as a great moral teacher, but I don't accept His claim to be God.' That is the one thing we must not say. A man who was merely a man and said the sort of things Jesus said would not be a great moral teacher. He would either be a lunatic—on a level with the man who says he is a poached egg—or else he would be the Devil of Hell. You must make your choice. Either this man was, and is, the Son of God: or else a madman or something worse."[10]

In this chapter we have tried to get some perspective on the eternal Word, the Bible, and the living Word, Jesus Christ. Now we shall find out what Christ and Scripture tell us about death: what it really is, when it started, what transpires after physical death, what the Bible says about escape from the final clutches of death, and the hope that God has made available to man.

TWELVE
THE ETERNAL DAY

C. S. Lewis, a gifted scholar, professor at Cambridge, and man of letters, who once described himself, converted while in his forties, as "the most reluctant and dejected convert in all of England," said something once that pierced my heart. Having just returned from India, I was in London in the autumn of 1971, reading a sermon entitled "The Weight of Glory," given by Lewis at Oxford. The words, I would learn, were not the wild, unbridled theologizings of an overdeveloped literary imagination trying to compensate for a meager exposure to biblical knowledge; rather, they were based on a profound and systematic awareness of the permutations of Scripture. Lewis's exegesis, hermeneutics, and systematic theology were exactly right, and his literary genius propelled these truths with a vividness lacking in many theologians.

> It is a serious thing to live in a society of possible gods and goddesses, to remember that the dullest and most uninteresting person you can talk to may one day be a creature which, if you saw it now, you would be strongly tempted to worship, or else a horror and a corruption such as you now meet, if at all, only in a nightmare. All day long we are, in some degree, helping each other to one or other of these destinations.... There are no ordinary people. You have never talked to a mere mortal.

Nations, cultures, arts, civilizations—these are mortal, and their life is to ours as the life of a gnat. But it is immortals whom we joke with, work with, marry, snub, and exploit—immortal horrors or everlasting splendors.[1]

If I had left Hyde Park and walked to the borough of London known as Westminster, I would have seen etched on an old wall that great confession of faith drawn up four hundred years before Lewis by that assembly of Christians who carefully prooftexted, with a jealous reverence, their confession of faith, the Westminster Confession.

The Westminster Assembly had such a high regard for Scripture that they dared not stray even a jot or a tittle from the clear declarations of biblical revelation. They would add or subtract *nothing* from Scripture's declaration, for they knew that by doing so they would jeopardize their very souls for eternity (see Rev. 22:19). They dared not handle "the word of God deceitfully" (2 Cor. 4:2).

Had I read what they had written, I would have found "The Eternal Day," in chapter 32 of the confession, where men become "immortal horrors or everlasting splendors."

> The bodies of men, after death, return to dust, and see corruption: (Gen. 3:19; Acts 13:36) but their souls, which neither die nor sleep, having an immortal substance, immediately return to God who gave them: (Luke 23:43; Eccles. 12:7) the souls of the righteous, being then made perfect in holiness, are received in the highest heavens, where they behold the face of God, in light and glory, waiting for the full redemption of their bodies. (Heb. 12:23; II Cor. 5:1, 6, 8; Phil. 1:23; Acts 3:21; Eph. 4:10; Rom. 8:23). And the souls of the wicked are cast into hell; where they remain in torments and utter darkness, reserved to the judgment of the great day. (Luke 16:23, 24; Acts 1:25; Jude 6, 7; I Pet. 3:19). Beside these two places, for souls separated from the bodies, the Scripture acknowledgeth none.
>
> At the last day, such as are found alive shall not die, but be changed: (I Thess. 4:17; I Cor. 15:51,52) and all the

dead shall be raised up, with the selfsame bodies, and none other (although with different qualities), which shall be united again to their souls forever (John 5:25-29; Acts 24:15; Job 19:26, 27; Dan. 12:2; I Cor. 15:42-44).

The bodies of the unjust shall, by the power of Christ, be raised to dishonor; the bodies of the just, by His Spirit, unto honor; and be made conformable to His own glorious body. (Acts 24:15; John 5:25-29; I Cor. 15:43; Phil. 3:21).[2]

This banner of the great Reformation, which characterized the era of Calvin, Luther, Knox, and Whitefield, is a most careful distilling of the foundations of the Christian faith. Chapter 33, the last chapter, compasses the final judgment. Like the rest of the confession, it is derived from a clear lining up of hundreds of key Scriptures, according to context, intent, and meaning. Since it pertains to all of creation, it is wise to read it:

God hath appointed a day, wherein He will judge the world, in righteousness, by Jesus Christ (Acts 17:31), to whom all power and judgment is given of the Father. (John 5:22, 27). In which day, not only the apostate angels shall be judged (Jude 6; II Pet. 2:4), but likewise all persons that have lived upon earth shall appear before the tribunal of Christ, to give an account of their thoughts, words, and deeds; and to receive according to what they have done in the body, whether good or evil (II Cor. 5:10; Eccles. 12:14; Rom. 14:10, 12; Matt. 12:36, 37).

The end of God's appointing this day is for the manifestation of the glory of His mercy, in the eternal salvation of the elect; and of His justice, in the damnation of the reprobate, who are wicked and disobedient. For then shall the righteous go into everlasting life, and receive the fulness of joy and refreshing, which shall come from the presence of the Lord: but the wicked, who know not God, and obey not the gospel of Jesus Christ, shall be cast into eternal torments, and be punished with everlasting destruction from the presence of the Lord, and from the glory of His power (Matt. 25:31-46; Rom. 2:5,6; Rom. 9:22, 23; Matt. 25:21; Acts 3:19; II Thess. 1:7-10; Mark 9:48).[3]

This pronouncement is so weighty that as a rule people cover their ears in protest to escape its impact. It is the one fact of Scripture that people detest the most and try to forget as quickly as possible. Yet no evangelist is honest if he wishes to push people gently into the Kingdom of heaven with tinsel and trinkets while ignoring or being ashamed of the eternal day. It is there, and none can ignore it, for it will come as surely as the rising sun. The tendency to banish it by warping it into a stereotype and then utterly despising it is common. I did that most of my life. Yet often I got the most unsettled feeling when the remnants of my conscience, which I had all but subdued, would occasionally rise up to protest. Meanwhile, my mind raced to find viable alternatives, saying, "I thought I had disposed of you once and for all; yet you come back to haunt me like a ghost."

The ultimate solution is not the Zen Koan, the primal scream, the up-front commune style, the transactional group's total encounter, or the transcendent samadhi; it is to look directly at the bare facts of God. It is the ultimate epistemological problem. I spent a painful childhood observing past masters and adepts sidestep this problem with some of the most complex diversions, stratagems, and psychological games. What the human mind can devise to escape this reality is almost awesome. Because this, far above the ego death of the East, requires a true change of oneself and true humility, it is known as "conversion." Few are willing to give up their own private claims on their lives, and they will not admit the tenacity with which they are holding on to life, or their strong wills for what they want their lives to be. This is called "impenitence."

Aldous Huxley once said that he never really had an intellectual problem with Christianity; he had a moral one, for he did not deny the facts or the inevitable sense they made. Likewise, there may be a thousand synods whose aim it is to change the simple truth and evolve some new insight; there may be a new papal bull or some inner echelon which claims special revelation. But the fact remains, "The word of our God endures forever" (Isa. 40:8, TEV). The pages of Scripture are open, plain for all to see. If we look at all of the major confessions regarding the eternal day, they fully agree. Why? It is like a logical syllogism. God has made sure the propositions of Scripture can hold only one true configuration, whether analyzed prayerfully or run through a computer. The eternal day always emerges.

The only way to knock the configuration out of shape is to symbolize everything, as Paul Tillich and Rudolf Bultmann have, or to say that the biblical source is invalid and therefore open to private editorializing, at which point one takes a few select bits of Scripture willy-nilly to prove anything he wants. With a black enough editorial pencil, one can syncretize Christianity with anything.

Yet the mind uses other tricks to obscure the truth; the caricature is the most popular. (Remember Moody reminding us of angels and harps?) For example, someone says to himself, God truly did a wonderful thing by creating a cosmos of so many parsecs of intergalactic space, with distant quasars and infinite stars. When I picture the final judgment, my imagery constantly encompasses something like the local high school auditorium, with someone like the principal sitting center stage under a bare light bulb, beneath mold-covered curtains, while looking out at a most unimpressive assortment of people. Perhaps on the sidelines are a few kids made up as angels, with (you guessed it) harps, sequins, gossamer robes, and metallic bronze face cream.

We think of the cosmos, and our minds leap out forever; we think of the eternal day, and we picture it as occurring at the local civic center. Since the vision is not feasible, we reject the whole concept as primitive. We have just dealt deceitfully with the Word of God. Such stereotypes have so deeply invaded our minds that to see beyond them requires true Christian enlightenment. For one thing, it means discarding a host of sixteenth-century paintings which we mentally overlay on Scripture. But in the process we must not deny the report of Scripture and gnosticize it into a higher mystical message. Paul anticipated this problem in his battle against the Gnostics. The apostle was most literal:

But if there is no resurrection of the dead, then Christ has not been raised; if Christ has not been raised, then our preaching is in vain and your faith is in vain. We are even found to be misrepresenting God, because we testified of God that he raised Christ, whom he did not raise if it is true that the dead are not raised. For if the dead are not raised, your faith is futile and you are still in your sins. Then those also who have fallen asleep in Christ have perished. If for this life only we have hoped in Christ, we are of all men most to be pitied (1 Cor. 15:13-19, RSV).

Paul was not dealing with Brahman or hazy balls of light or disembodied beings of light. He was talking about the resurrected Christ, to whom Thomas cried out, "My Lord and my God" (John 20:28). If Christ were a ball of light, that is how he would have appeared to his waiting disciples and to the crowd of five hundred. We must realize that there is something of far greater immensity than balls of light in the plan of God's new heaven. We have to compass the fact of "glorified bodies" in a context far more splendid than we have ever experienced here on earth. The problem does not lie in the revelation of God, but in our ability to visualize: "Eye hath not seen, nor ear heard, neither have entered into the heart of man, the things which God hath prepared for them that love him" (1 Cor. 2:9).

Scripture, then, has told us something; it is beyond us to visualize the eternal day, as beyond us as a blind man trying to picture the three primary colors and their infinite variations, not to speak of the Moghul Gardens of Kashmir. He cannot. For that matter, nor can an ant comprehend Mahler's Tenth Symphony, scoping the vast range of feeling and complexity from the light violins to symphonic thunder, from pathos to adoration. Perhaps its antennae feel a thunderous rumble like that of a stampeding herd of cattle, but that is far from the sublime heart of Mahler's genius. So it is with us and eternity.

Therefore, what we have is a fundamental question regarding the nature of ultimate reality. Either creation will groan and travail forever, only finding release in the realm of the spirit, with good and evil coexisting, endless Chicagos passing by, civilizations replacing civilizations, a million dictatorships coming and going, and Lake Erie being filtered and repurified endless times (if the world goes on as it is, its decay is indefinite, according to the second law of thermodynamics), or the One who made it must change all that exists to make it other than what it is. If we deny matter and call it evil, if we opt for the realm of the spirit as did the Gnostics whom Paul opposed, as do the spiritualists, we are proclaiming a definite view concerning material reality. "It must be transcended," we are saying.

But the Bible says no. Material creation fell at a terrible price. God made the material universe and declared it "good," but he is not finished; the drama is not over yet. He can and will change His travailing creation, as he promised, within the twinkling of an eye. "It is good," the Bible says, not the accident of a half-baked plan. True, man has mangled it, but look at the luminous green of a tropical leaf, the Alps of Austria, or the emerald shores of Malabar and tell me that the prototypes from which they come are evil, an expensive accident. Even after millenia of creation being in third gear, according to the biblical model, and even though these are shadows of the original types, they still take your breath away. Some say the Creator goofed? No, man goofed.

Either creation will groan and travail forever, only finding release in the realm of the spirit, or God is deeply serious about his purpose to intervene in the created universe at the appointed time and change everything in the most radical way. Peter says,

> It is not that he is dilatory about keeping his own promise as some men seem to think; the fact is that he is very patient with you. He has no wish that any man should be destroyed; he wishes that all men should find the way to repentance. Yet the day of the Lord will come as unexpectedly as a thief. In that day the heavens will vanish in a tearing blast, the very elements will disintegrate in heat and the earth and all its works will disappear (2 Pet. 3:9, 10, Phillips).

This matter of the new creation is discussed many times. The new creation follows the destruction of the old. But the question arises, Who will make it through the sieve? Will microbes and massage parlors hustle their way through with a sheepish smile? Not likely.

The prospect of the new creation is staggering. What we have seen in only a mere glimpse of Eden will appear with manifest power, stretching across eternity, a symphony of matter and spirit unlike anything we know, in total congress with the eternal, spotless, and perfect God, through Christ, the cornerstone of the created universe.

What of tears and lamentation? No more. What of bloated bodies in the Hudson River? You've heard it—the ten-year-old girl sitting on her Beverly Hills porch watching her cat. The next minute a van pulls up and hustles her away to New York to be in a porno white-slave ring, where she is raped and then butchered (it is happening now). Later, her body is found bleached white in the docks of Hoboken. Never again. How God hates that! Do you think he is jesting when he speaks of hell?

What of the cancers, poisons, pus-spewing wounds of our race, with its secret, burning inner cankers, its God-hating blindness and cruelties, its complicated truth-denying games? Do you not know that since man's fall, God has pronounced the sentence, "The [human] heart is deceitful above all things, and desperately wicked: who can know it?" (Jer. 17:9). So you're a good guy? A deep enough scalpel will show the Dr. Jekyll and Mr. Hyde nature of the most decent citizen. Beneath the whitewashed tomb is the most grotesque distortion of perfection. Will the Mr. Hyde in you make it through the sieve? If so, why did the Messiah come into the world to go through infinite agony? That is a deep question. Have you really considered it?

A slag heap will be banished across an infinite void, and then forgotten forever by the Godhead. Though a void, it will not be an impersonal state, for it will most definitely contain personalities—those to whom God, love, truth, and goodness were a blotch across the sky. In the end, they will be given their own domain. As self-proclaimed gods of their own universe, they will reap the fruits of their own willful autonomy: of unending remorse and pain, for "the smoke of their torment ascendeth up for ever" (Rev. 14:11). Surely you have read of these people in Dickens, and you've seen many of their names in the New York Times. They are all around you. Indeed, even now you may be in their ranks, if the Mr. Hyde nature in you has not yet been purged by the grace of God. Mr. Hydes do not pass into eternity to reign with God.

Consider the Word of God:

> Then I saw a great white throne and him who sat upon it; from his presence earth and sky fled away, and no place was found for them. And I saw the dead, great and small, standing before the throne, and books were opened. Also another book was opened, which is the book of life. And the dead were judged by what was written in the books, by what they had done. And the sea gave up the dead in it, Death and Hades gave up the dead in them, and all were judged by what they had done. Then Death and Hades were thrown into the lake of fire. This is the second death, the lake of fire; and if any one's name was not found written in the book of life, he was thrown into the lake of fire (Rev. 20:11-15, RSV).

Is it fair or right to minimize hell, especially when Jesus Christ himself talked about it in thirty-eight different places in the Gospel of Matthew alone? I am not being your friend if I say, "Don't worry" as you are about to do the equivalent of ushering your Jewish family on an unmarked Nazi train headed for Auschwitz, all because I don't want to spoil your mood. Equal enemies with the Nazis of the Jews in wartime Germany were those who suppressed the rumors of what was happening in the Third Reich. They were false peacemakers, and millions died as a result. The very Jews who might have escaped the holocaust stayed on with a false sense of assurance, only to be arrested by the Gestapo in midnight raids.

Those who have judged the Bible and mythologized hell to ease their minds have done the equivalent. They are telling you a different story than the one the Bible proclaims. In hundreds of places in both the Old Testament and the New Testament, God speaks of Gehenna and Sheol. If you declare this a mere myth, you are resting your soul on your own huge intuitive proclamation.

Yet the Bible was not a flash in the pan that came and went

like a thousand fads. It stuck. It is not a novel twist or a new breakthrough or a new peculiarity. Like Christ, it is "the same yesterday and today and for ever" (Heb. 13:8, RSV). (Just think, the very date on your birth certificate, or on your newspaper, is based on the advent of Christ.) If it were less, it could not be absolute truth. Yet people who summarily dismiss the Bible—which has survived thirty-five centuries and turned civilizations on their heads—even though they have never read it, will rest their eternal souls (and future bodies) on a "discovery" of Seth or on John Doe's "death experience."

Think of it, someone grabs a thin, new, little book, and believes John Doe's death account above the words of the great men of God who lived across a span of many centuries, who saw world empires change, and whom God chose to be his mouthpieces. Those men worked miracles and their moral quality of life was astounding. A modern reader will question the Bible in an instant, but he will gladly gulp down every tidbit about astral planes, beings of light, and chariots of the gods. Never would it occur to him that his faith rides on a far more flimsy string than is warranted, and not a single John Doe lay in a tomb for four days, as did Lazarus, in the stench of decaying flesh.

Raise a Lazarus and we have a miracle. But with John Doe the needle floated, the EEG floated, the watch ticked away from three to ten minutes, and clinicians yelled, "Dead." Old John revived and they proclaimed in all their wisdom, "Indeed, the machines say he died, so he must have truly died." It does not cross the mind of the reader, who is so cautious about the Bible, that John Doe's case is an index of the inadequacies of the clinical method in determining death. So I say, let the good doctor find us a man like Lazarus who has been dead for four days, and interview him, someone who is stone cold and in rigor mortis. Till then, I shall lean in the direction of Scripture.

Another thing the Bible says: you cannot any more sit at a séance and summon Uncle Rex than you can dip a fishing pole into the water at Dover, England, and pull in the same little gray fish you would if you fished in Miami. "But it looks the same." Indeed it does.

In the Gospel of Luke, Christ gives us a significant lesson.

Do not allow imagery like "Abraham's bosom" to throw you, unless you are willing to do a word study on Hebrew origins; it is a most real and apropos term. This settles the matter of the "impassable barrier." But again, do not grab onto the vehicle of the story, the imagery or the setting, to invalidate it unless you are willing to undertake the scholarship required to intelligently comprehend and critique it.

> Now there was a certain rich man, and he habitually dressed in purple and fine linen, gaily living in splendor every day. And a certain poor man named Lazarus was laid at his gate, covered with sores, and longing to be fed with the crumbs which were falling from the rich man's table; besides, even the dogs were coming and licking his sores. Now it came about that the poor man died and he was carried away by the angels to Abraham's bosom; and the rich man also died and was buried. And in Hades he lifted up his eyes, being in torment, and saw Abraham far away, and Lazarus in his bosom. And he cried out and said, "Father Abraham, have mercy on me, and send Lazarus, that he may dip the tip of his finger in water and cool off my tongue; for I am in agony in this flame." But Abraham said, "Child, remember that during your life you received your good things, and likewise Lazarus bad things; but now he is being comforted here, and you are in agony. And besides all this, between us and you there is a great chasm fixed, in order that those who wish to come over from here to you may not be able, and that none may cross over from there to us." And he said, "Then I beg you, Father, that you send him to my father's house—for I have five brothers—that he may warn them, lest they also come to this place of torment." But Abraham said, "They have Moses and the Prophets; let them hear them." But he said, "No, Father Abraham, but if someone goes to them from the dead, they will repent!" But he said to him, "If they do not listen to Moses and the Prophets, neither will they be persuaded if someone rises from the dead" (Luke 16:19-31, NASB).

Needless to say, Christ's teaching here is rich with truths, and should be read again and again. Nevertheless, the main fact for us at this point is the statement, "Between us and you there is a great chasm fixed, in order that those who wish to come over from here to you may not be able, and that none may cross over from there to us." In short, the barrier is impassable between them, not to speak of between them and the living. So who is showing up at the séances and on the Ouija boards? Other forms of spirits, as we have observed in earlier chapters.

Yet another truth emerges from the above teaching which we should not let escape us. If men are not persuaded in their hearts by the simple truth of Scripture, "neither will they be persuaded if someone rises from the dead." This is a profound statement on the human condition. Remember, hordes of people saw the Red Sea part, crossed into the wilderness with Moses, and drank from springs in the desert opened up by the staff of Moses, but later they actually renounced what they had seen in order to make and worship a golden calf at the base of Mount Sinai. The miracles did not change their hearts permanently. People are enraptured for a while, but often the feeling melts away. The **truth,** however, remains and is changeless.

The central question at this point is, What is death? To answer it, we must ask, What does God say of death? What do we learn from the hundreds of verses in the Bible?

Death is the "final enemy" to be cast into "the lake of fire," and it was the first curse. Balanced on a perfectly free decision at a particular time and place in history, death entered like an infinite garbage dump on a pellucid mountain lake. In a trice, its impact reverberated across all creation. By free will, Adam opted for the promise of knowledge "to be as a god" and, as a consequence, lost his very real kingship of this world. The succeeding king, according to the Bible, is called "the prince of this world" (John 12:31). The one who pulled the greatest con job ever on the two perfect people is also the author of death's entry into our domain of existence, and his name is Satan. That is what the Bible says.

Physical death has been the most apparent feature of death,

and it has reigned across the centuries. But that is only the tip of the iceberg, for there is more to death than physical destruction or entropy. More terrible was the immediate void created, the literal disfellowshiping with the living God. Our entire nature was reamed out in a moment, and we as a people were changed utterly within. We became depraved. Were God without mercy, we would have been consumed in the fire of judgment then and there (but, you see, there was this matter of the promised Messiah, Jesus Christ).

A perfect universe, as God originally made it, knows nothing of the unending wastage and agony of death. Death serves no purpose in such a universe. It is contradictory to the character of the eternal, holy, and perfect God to create perfect images of himself in a physical medium, only to have them melt away into grotesque caricatures reminiscent of Dorian Gray. Remember, he who made billions of galaxies can quite capably sustain an eternal body in his creation. He can do it. But we forget this.

All we have ever known in our present experience is death reigning in a fallen universe, creation travailing in third gear. So since death is everywhere, we conclude that it must be the status quo of all existence and all conceivable existence. But God's revelation disagrees. It did not start out that way. Disbelieve if you will—because your ability to conceive of this hampers you—but that does not alter the fact. God did not make man in his image to die! God himself declares this.

The Bible speaks of three forms of death: spiritual, physical, and eternal death. "The Bible does not know the distinction, so common among us, between a physical, spiritual, and an eternal death; it has a synthetic view of death and regards it as separation from God."[4] We think of it as the cessation of existence. The Bible speaks of death as the cessation of our connection with the eternal God. Now that puts us in a new ball park. "The wages of sin is death" (Rom. 6:23).

1. *Spiritual death.* Our souls are cut off from God. We are born that way, and this is the condition in which a majority of people eke out their shoddy existence apart from the Messiah (Eph. 2:1, 5, 12; 4:18). They are desolate, hollow, empty, alone, afraid, willful, perverse, antagonistic, and stained in

every sense of the word. This is how the Bible defines death working in our very lives (Gen. 6:5; Rom. 7:18). Our consciences constantly testify against us, while a general dread of punishment fills our hearts. We have guilt and are polluted. In the sight of God we are unrighteous and unholy, which is manifested in our thoughts, words, and deeds. Our position is an active principle in life, like an unending stream of poison invading a clear mountain spring. Therefore, the soul is a battlefield of conflicting passions, thoughts, and desires. Harmony of life is destroyed, and pain is the real companion in our suffering state. Christ proclaimed that we are bondslaves of sin.

2. *Physical death*. Perhaps one of the cruelest things I could do would be to walk along a long shoreline with a corkscrew and grab one conch after another, pulling them out of their shells and leaving them writhing on barnacle-covered rocks, and then, with hammer and pliers, rip the shells indiscriminately off turtles and snails. The point is, to have the whole creature, we need the shell as well. Just part of it does not work.

Man is not a bodiless spirit or a spiritless body. For God to restore man as man is to make him wholly man, not just a spirit. The abnormal condition is to have the spirit ripped from its flesh. This is part of the curse of death. The ultimate state is the restoration of the whole man, which will occur on the eternal day. We wait for the memory of God to reassemble those who lived. It will happen.

Just as surely as the original models of Leonardo da Vinci's machines have been duplicated down to the last nail and wire by reading the original plans, he who holds the atoms in place to form a trillion crystal lattices here and so many mountains there, can do the same in reassembling us who have existed in the flesh, whom he created in the first place.

That physical death is lamentable is evidenced as we see Christ at the tomb of Lazarus. "Jesus wept" (John 11:35). To have the crown of God's creation divided asunder unnaturally, the body rotting and the spirit temporarily amputated, is more of an abomination, an indignity, than it would be to have the beaches coated with deshelled mollusks.

3. *Eternal death.* "This may be regarded as the culmination and completion of spiritual death. The restraints of the present fall away, and the corruption of sin has its perfect work. The full weight of the wrath of God descends on the condemned. Their separation from God, the source of life and joy, is complete, and this means death in the most awful sense of the word. Their outward condition is made to correspond with the inward state of their evil souls. There are pangs of conscience, and physical pain. 'And the smoke of their torment goeth up for ever and ever' (Rev. 14:11)."[5]

This state of eternal death follows the judgment on the great day. We do not see the last of death at somebody's funeral. That is just a stage, not the true end. When we say that death is a curse, quoting the Bible, it means literally that it is a curse. You do not wash it away any easier than you wash off burning napalm. Wake up!

Is it lightly, then, that Paul booms out with a rejoining shout, "O death, where is thy victory? O death, where is thy sting?" (1 Cor. 15:55, RSV; Paul quoting Isa. 25:8). Can we fathom the deep plan of the Overcomer, and the depth of the "final enemy," death? Death tugs relentlessly, for it is intertwined in the deepest fabric of our lives. It is no small miracle, then, for Christ to raise all of mankind, to say, "I am the resurrection and the life; he who believes in me, though he die, yet shall he live" (John 11:25, 26, RSV).

Perhaps to illustrate his point, soon after this declaration Christ called into the tomb of the man who had been dead for four days. The man Lazarus emerged; he would live the remainder of his life as a normal man. The Bible does not record even a hint of some discorporated sojourn into the realm of spirits, though the opportunity was amply there if ever there were a time to do it. Instead, the Bible assures us of something else: Lazarus is to be with Christ forever; and on the eternal day, all who are "in Christ" will stand with Lazarus, not as spirits, but as resurrected, glorified creatures with bodies of immutable beauty, containing the innate power to survive for eternity.

No, our bodies will not be exactly flesh and blood; they cannot be what they are here (see 1 Cor. 15:50). But the idea comes to mind that for those bodies to inherit eternity, the contrast between them and our present bodies. [...] are now more like the supposed phantoms, ar[...] bodies will be the real bodies, the substantiv[...] who live in the land of shadows, as C. S. Lewi[s...] brilliant allegory, *The Great Divorce*. To spec[ulate beyond the] clear statements of Scripture would be folly.

Who is this One who has conquered death across the ages? Who is the real Christ? That is what I asked in a small south Indian hotel room right before I met him and was converted, after two years in India as a foremost disciple of a miracle-working, self-proclaimed messiah. When I called out, two thousand years after his advent, it was Christ himself who entered my life. I was healed in mind and spirit in a manner that no other encounter in my life has come near. I got up from my knees with a totally new orientation, a new heart, mind, and values; a sense of hope, a sense of joy. As I came to know the Scriptures in the following years, I knew why. To change a single life is a miracle. To see the record of millions of lives changed through this One, Christ, during the last two thousand years, is an undeniable miracle.

We are talking about the real Christ of Scripture, the sovereign Lord before whom " 'every knee shall bow,' ... And 'every tongue shall confess' that Jesus Christ is the Lord" (Phil. 2:10-11, Phillips). We are not talking about a mythologized, gnostic, or spiritualized Christos, some so-called higher master. Remember, the Bible predicts many false Christs.

The true Christ of Scripture is the Christ of history, the One foretold in 332 specific prophecies in the Old Testament.[6] Among those prophecies are those of his nativity (Isa. 9:6); his Bethlehem birthplace (Mic. 5:2); his descent into Egypt (Hos. 11:1); the massacre of innocents (Jer. 31:15); his ministry in Galilee (Isa. 9:1,2); his rejection by the Jews (Psa. 2:1; 22:12; 41:5; 69:8); his persecution (Psa. 22:6; Isa. 49:7; 53:3); his betrayal for thirty pieces of silver (Zech. 11:12); and his desertion by his disciples (Zech. 13:7).

If we examine the Christ of history we have left the realm of myths. In his wake we see a world turned upside down, and the shock waves continue. The early church spilled out their lives by the tens of thousands, not for a myth, but for One who aid to them, "Behold my hands and feet, that it is I myself: handle me, and see; for a spirit hath not flesh and bones, as ye see me have" (Luke 24:39). He is the One whom Job anticipated over a thousand years earlier, when he said, "I know that my redeemer liveth, and that he shall stand at the latter day upon the earth: and though after my skin worms destroy this body, yet in my flesh shall I see God" (Job 19:25, 26). More than 85 specific and fairly extensive references to bodily resurrection are in the New Testament.[7] It is a cornerstone of biblical Christianity, and those who argue around it are opposing the Christ of history.

Where do we tangibly see death defeated by the Christ of history? Where was his role as Savior completed? If God's greatest effort throughout history was to produce the Messiah, not by bludgeoning the world but by the most careful loving plan, the mission of Christ was crucial. Meanwhile, the opposition throughout history has seemed staggering; consider Moses riding history's course on a papyrus raft, or that single family of Noah's escaping the deluge, or Joseph and Mary fleeing into Egypt with the young Jesus. Remember, if all of the family lines across any age could have been cut off or polluted, that also would have annihilated the messianic line, made God's word untrue (an impossibility), and therefore, by history, made God un-God. Who do you think is behind this kind of deep thinking and planning?

The greatest wail in the history of mankind occurred at the cross of Christ, but it was not Christ who was wailing; it was that terrible genius, the former "illuminated one," who had played cosmic chess with God. What happened on that hill of Golgotha overlooking Jerusalem? The debt of sin of the human race was erased, making possible reconciliation with God. If humanity looked lost and forever cut off from God, now there was the doorway into redemption, not for a few, but for a great multitude, as was promised to Abraham.

For a moment the event on the hill looked like the destruction of God's plan, until what had really happened entered the mind of the adversary. Then the terrible realization must have hit, akin to the defeat of Napoleon, where for an instant he owned the empires of the world as he saw the remnants of a conquered army. The next moment he looked about and, on all sides, looming on the hilltops, were the immense garrisons of the enemy. The tables had utterly turned.

This sounds simple, but it is deep. God is infinitely honest, infinitely just. Therefore, he cannot base the universe on truth and mend it with lies. If a house has burned down, it has burned down. You build it again from scratch; you do not cross it off the record and say it never was there, or daydream it away. If you do, your foundations were not of truth. When a perfect man, Adam, brought sin into existence in our world, it took the exact counterpayment for sin (death) of a totally perfect Man to satisfy the laws of the Creator and reverse what had happened (i. e., legitimately build another house). None but Christ has been perfect and sinless. This sinless Messiah fulfilled the prophecy in Isaiah and died to save his people. On that cross an ultimate solution was arrived at which would mean eternal bliss for those of us who would entrust our lives to him; it means the impossible for us—entering the light in fellowship with the eternal God, whose brilliance pales the light of a billion suns.

A fact of history is staring us straight in the face. When they brought Christ's body down from the cross before the eyes of Israel, the people knew well the prophecy that the Messiah was to rise again. The Sanhedrin knew it, the priests knew it, and the Pharisees and Sadducees knew it, as did the common people. Caiaphas and Pontius Pilate knew it. So what was the plan? Cap the tomb with an immense boulder, seal it with the seal of state, and place a Roman or temple guard in front of the tomb (they did). Then, to really drive their point home, when the three days had elapsed, their task would be simple enough: to parade the mangled corpse of Jesus through the streets. That would annihilate belief in him forever. But there was the matter of an empty tomb. Then a band of frightened men became bold. Only then did those disciples risk their own lives, for they had walked and talked with their risen Lord.

CONCLUSION

At the outset of this book, we saw in "Sudden Death" what is supposed to take place at death, according to the latest "scientific breakthrough" of Moody and Kubler-Ross. This view is currently taking the nation by storm. This recent fascination with death and the wide popularity of this new model has spurred us to go on a wide search, not only to find what our modern death model most closely resembles, but what each of the traditions says and stands for. We have looked at the traditions of the psychics, mediums, and occultists; the yogis, Eastern mystics, and mystery religions; the Western thinkers, philosophers, scientists, and cosmic humanists; and finally we looked at biblical Christianity to see what Christ and the Bible really have to say about death.

Since we were aware that most of the above traditions claimed to be in allegiance with Christianity and often borrowed Christian terms, in our search we compared biblical passages with the various claims of the different traditions. At the end of our investigation we found that the Christian teaching on death is utterly unique and will not blend into these other beliefs. The ancient tradition and the biblical tradition stand opposed, and the gap between them is enormous; their views of death do not harmonize at all, but rather, are directly set against each other.

Immediately before we looked into the teachings of the

psychics and mediums, we tried to find an acceptable definition for death. This brought into question whether any of Moody's subjects had in fact died at all. The case seemed to be that the machines and clinicians had misdiagnosed death, and that the experiences reported by Moody's subjects were perhaps due to other causes than death, perhaps something closer to the dream state had been approached, or some physiological event had affected them. But the pattern of their reports seemed unusual.

Looking into the world of psychics and mediums, we saw that their tradition stems from ancient Babylon. Immediately we found that biblical passages sternly warn against mediumship and familiar spirits. The revelations among mediums and psychics, such as Cayce, Ford, and Roberts, all varied along similar but confusing lines. As opposed to the prophets of the Bible, the mediums often were morally debased, hostile to God, and in the grip of a force which was clearly not altogether good. We noted a profound similarity between the modern Moody—Kubler-Ross model of death and what the psychics teach. In the candid confessions of Raphael Gasson, an ex-medium from London, we saw an explicit one-for-one correspondence between the death reports in *Life After Life* and the major tenets of the World-wide Church of Spiritualism, a connection too uncanny to be accidental. Then we discovered that Kubler-Ross herself used mediums and had her own spirit guide named Salem. Having known Moody personally, I knew he was by no means naive regarding the tenets of spiritualism, but had been a quiet seeker for years. To what did the Bible and Gasson attribute the experiences of Moody's subjects and the mediums? The deceptive powers of evil.

We considered the mystics and yogis of the East and traced many of their teachings back to ancient Babylon, where we saw the ancient priesthood, the divine-within concept, reincarnation, self-evolution, the psychic sciences such as astrology, and the idea of man becoming God. It became clear that the teachings of the psychics led directly into this view of reality. We discovered that the heart of the Eastern tradition—that the higher self is one with God—is the essence of the Genesis lie given to Eve in the Bible. The East portrayed death as a release and a dear friend, but the terrible facts of life in India today brought the fruits of this belief into question, and the biblical tradition was clearly antithetical to the Eastern view.

Turning to the West, we saw a Western world in an identity crisis. The West was ready to leap from the philosophy of "scientism" right into mysticism, without a second thought. As we peered into the past to look at the foundations of Western philosophy, we saw what had happened. Centuries ago, in the name of objective truth, God and the Bible had been thrown out the window, leaving a large gap in man's soul. Existentialism and despair grew as a mood. But there were still large questions, which science and rationalism and the philosophies after rationalism had not answered, and man's world had become no better. Man, believing in the Kantian notion that no unified field of knowledge connecting the physical with the spiritual was possible, became desperate and started to look for any convenient doorways to escape the constant hum of existential despair. That opened the doors for Tim Leary, the gurus, psychedelia, Castaneda, and the new mystics. The setting in our culture became ideal for the reception of the new "scientific breakthrough" concerning death offered by Moody and Kubler-Ross.

Finally, as many are beginning to do today, we turned to the Bible. Science and philosophy have in no way been able to dispose of the Bible. Upon investigation, it turns out to be the most incredible book on earth. God's powerful words say that death is not a dear old friend, but an ancient enemy, and that there is but a single escape from the curse of death: Jesus Christ. The alternative is truly terrible.

After considering the Bible, it became even more clear that not one of the other traditions truly accepts the biblical view of death without redefining concepts and terms and then squeezing them through a special filtering system. The Bible's potent, startling, frightening, and potentially hopeful statements have been blurred, if not obliterated, by the other traditions. Those traditions have disposed of the transcendent, holy, and personal God of the Bible while shifting the balances of good, evil, and morality. They also have deftly disposed of the most threatening thought for all mankind:

eternal hell, about which the Bible warns both compassionately and sternly. But in expunging hell, they also have jettisoned eternal heaven, with its immensity, bliss, and grandeur.

What do we say now about driving a car and fantasizing a death experience, as in "Sudden Death"? In the end, this breakthrough by Moody and Kubler-Ross to solve the riddle of death offers little more than a trifling, phantasmagoric, palisades park alternative to the biblical heaven. The imagery they give does not need to be caricatured; it serves as its own bleak caricature, with its pastel colors, amorphous forms, and smoky encounters. Even without the biblical perspective to guide us, to see death painted with such saccharine benignity, winking at us behind a honeycomb smile, has too much of the chilling effect of a "setup" to really be convincing. Something does not feel right underneath the reassuring background melodies, the reception-room smiles, and the clinical aerosol fragrance. One still gets the feeling that something foreboding is behind the door of the Moody—Kubler-Ross reception office, some terrible machination reminiscent of the Frankenstein story.

Who are these beings of light with their effervescent cheerfulness? When unmasked, what are these "old friends" like? I believe we would discover the very thing Moody and Kubler-Ross are most quick to dismiss: that the being of light was among the legions of "wicked potentates" and "cosmic powers of evil" that the Apostle Paul refers to in Ephesians 6. Make no mistake, the only possible biblical explanation for these beings of light is that they are demons masquerading as cosmic nice guys. And do not assume that some of these researchers have not had the same chilling thought.

Since we are now opening a spiritual "can of worms," I will mention a brilliantly written book, *Hostage to the Devil*, released recently, which deals with the subject of demonic influences on human lives.[1] Steeped in mature and deep insight, it was written by Malachi Martin, the religion editor of *The National Review*. Martin, a former professor and Oxford scholar, is a Christian. Two relevant chapters are entitled "The Rooster and the Tortoise" and "Father Bones and Mr. Natch." The book is based on five recent cases of demon possession, one of which is about a man who until recently was a famous parapsychologist. The subtle and sweet quality of some of these spirit deceptions is awesome.

At this point, it is time to discuss the heart of the issue. Satan is no myth, despite his aptitude at demythologizing himself behind numerous respectable academic arguments and ethnic clichés. He is only too real and is a terrible, dark strength. The Bible states that as his time draws to a close, his campaign of deception will be pervasive, subtle, and ruthless. He is described as resembling a roaring lion out to devour the souls of men (see 1 Pet. 5:8). He hates Christ, and he hates you and me. The supreme genius of deception, he can use almost anything to achieve his end: myths, pipe dreams, fashionable philosophies of the day, literary poignancies, distractions, religions, psychic powers, gods, legends, and anything else which can act as a wedge between us and Christ. He even uses the computer and economics to gather power over human souls. Finally, he uses such palatable models of death as we encountered in "Sudden Death" to sweeten its bitter taste and drug our minds. He does this with a fair-minded, unbiased, benign, and humanitarian voice.

I now appeal to you to consider very soberly the immensity of your choice and its consequences as you decide what you really believe death to be. Death, you may find, could be the final seal of destiny. It is up to you to decide whether death for you will be with the genuine Christ or without him. Do not be surprised if it turns out that you only have one chance to find out.

APPENDIXES
by Robert Schlagal

APPENDIX ONE
The West:
The Great Revolt

Men . . . suppress the truth in unrighteousness, because that which is known about God is evident within them. . . . For since the creation of the world His invisible attributes, His eternal power and divine nature, have been clearly seen, being understood through what has been made, so that they are without excuse. For even though they knew God, they did not honor Him as God, or give thanks; but they became futile in their speculations, and their foolish heart was darkened (Rom. 1:18-21, NASB).

The changes wrought by the Age of Reason, the refrain runs, have had a profound effect upon the modern world. As a dynamic historical movement, this period more than any other had its roots deep in the thinking of its contemporary philosophers. It was an age filled with burgeoning energy and excitement as it pursued the new revolutionary humanistic dream. As a philosophic age, it was possessed of a unique messianic fervor born of a new vision of the sufficiency of the human mind and its undiscovered potentials. Such a secular utopianism as the later stages of the Enlightenment exhibited found natural expression in political unrest and in the revolutions, especially in France.

But more importantly for our interests here are new assumptions and conclusions about reality which were to disrupt the normative Christian understanding of the world and man's place in it. A group of thinkers called "the Continental Rationalists"—Descartes, Leibniz, and Spinoza—began their philosophic speculations from the autonomous mind of man, not from God or the objective world. Taken on faith was the mind's ability to function correctly, independent of any external guidelines for thought, and independent of God's statements about his creation. The mind could build a sound, unshakeable system of thought, they felt, by deductive reasoning from simple premises, reinforced by truths retained from the Judeo-Christian world view. Principally, God and the moral and physical order of the universe were kept as cornerstones, but God was changed from being the absolute Sovereign of the universe, without whom nothing could exist, to an *innate idea* within man's mind. Derived *from* and authenticated by man's mind, God was used to validate their deductions.

Descartes began building his rational philosophy from his single, indubitable truth: *"cogito, ergo sum,"* "I think, therefore I am." This was the single fact upon which no doubt could be shed. Having established man as the ultimate fact in the universe, the only unshakeable fact, he proceeded to "prove" the existence of God and, from him, the existence of the external world. In his popular book on existentialism, *Irrational Man*, William Barrett says of Descartes:

> By doubting all things Descartes arrived at a single certainty: the existence of his own consciousness—the famous *Cogito, ergo sum,* "I think, therefore I am." This is the point at which modern philosophy, and with it the modern epoch, begins: man is locked up in his own ego. Outside him is the doubtful world of things, which his science has now taught him are really not the least like their familiar appearances. Descartes got the external world back through a belief in God, who in His goodness would not deceive us into believing that this external world existed if it really did not. But the ghost of subjectivism (and solipsism too) is there and haunts the whole of modern philosophy.[1]

Regardless of how he felt privately about ultimate reality, it is obvious from Descartes' thinking that God and the created universe were being rendered dependent upon man for authentic existence.

Another group of philosophers took a further step toward "modernism" in thinking. In order to follow the strict guidelines of sense experience—their premise was that all knowledge was derived from experience—the British empiricists, Locke, Berkeley, and Hume, denied the existence of the innate ideas held by the rationalists. All that man can know must originate in experience. All "abstract ideas," such as God or truth or the like, must derive from some sense impression in order to be noetically valid.

Of the three philosophers, only David Hume explored the implications of a pure empiricism with unremitting vigor. All that man can legitimately know from experience, Hume concludes, is a succession of sensations. Because God and one's personal identity and the causal structure of the world (i.e., the orderly, connected patterns of events we know) are not immediate sense impressions, like pain or color or size, *we cannot know that they exist.* Man experiences only a succession of events which habit and memory lead him to connect with unifying structure. Because the sun always has been observed to rise in the east, we go beyond the limits of our experience and, out of habit, assume that it will continue to do so. Our experience, however, has no necessary connections with the future. No reliable knowledge can be derived from our experience if there are no real, necessary connections between events.

For Hume, knowledge is only possible in the most restricted sense. He cannot really assert that an external world exists; yet, despite the conclusions of such a reductive analysis, he is forced to admit that the practical demands of daily life require that the unverifiable order of nature be assumed. Barrett captures succinctly Hume's dilemma when the philosopher, "in a moment of acute skepticism, felt panicky in the solitude of his study and had to go out and join his friends in the billiard room in order to be reassured that the external world was really there."[2] He is left with a remarkable dichotomy between theory and practice. The results of his thinking remain inconsistent with the demands of life.

When Hume finished his empirical analysis, the possibility of scientific knowledge was in question. Immanuel Kant, shaken by Hume, sought to extract thinking from the impasse into which it had worked itself, and his solution laid the groundwork for thought in the nineteenth century, where the occult began to take firm root.

Kant's revolutionary move was this: in order to rescue science and philosophy from skepticism while at the same time preserving *humanistic* assumptions, Kant removed the form and structure of reality from their precarious place in a problematic external world and established them *within the mind of man*. The patterns which science studies, the dynamic orderliness of nature which rewards the efforts of science, are not the result of habit and custom, as Hume had argued; instead, Kant said, this order originates *in the observer*. This *subjective order* is the *condition for perception* itself.

This move of Kant's is crucial, for it philosophically and epistemologically throws the door open not only for a knowledge independent of God, but also for mysticism, monism, and pursuit of the occult. The nature of the mind, Kant argues, is to order the indeterminate stuff of sensation so that it can be perceived or known. This ordering occurs *before experience is possible*. Time, space, and causality are not "out there" in a real world; they are extended *from* the subject's mind *for* the act of perception. Science is successful in its generalizations about the normal relations between objects of experience because these relations are established a priori by what Kant called the forms and categories of human understanding which allow objective experience to occur. What reality is, what "things in themselves" are, cannot be known. What we "know" is made possible not by God, not by the mind's penetration of a real world, but by the mind's projection of what we can know upon an essentially unknowable world.

Speaking from a position much influenced by Kant, Samuel Taylor Coleridge, the nineteenth-century English poet, said that we half create, half receive the world, so that what man fabricates in perception cannot be separated from what is really there. Man knows only experience, not things in themselves. In a sense, the mind is like a film projector and the world a screen in terms of which man simultaneously creates and perceives. Or further, with an image Walt Whitman used, man is like a spider who spins the world he knows out of himself, for the world as we know it, Kant said, is a construct of our minds. The knowledge that man can have, then, is orderly and reliable (and independent of God), because it is ultimately extended from a creative human center.

Various philosophic problems have arisen and still persist as a result of these theories. Prior to the substitution of humanistic (man-centered) emergent trends for theistic (God-centered) epistemology and ontology, the significance of individual life was guaranteed. Time and history were intelligible and real phenomena; the fact that the universe exists was explained in a way that allowed for sustained intelligent inquiry because the vast patterned structures and dynamic energies of the universe are an outgrowth of God's wise and sovereign purpose; that is, form and structure were not projections, they were inherent in the reality of a knowable world. As God and his self-revelation were suppressed or directly denied, these facts (which normal perception takes for granted) became philosophically problematic, as has become increasingly apparent. Of what significance is the person in the scheme of Darwinism, Marxism, capitalism, or behaviorism? As we have moved further into modernity, even a system like democracy, which seeks to preserve and enhance human dignity, is engulfed by the universalist political machinery of our age: technocracy. It is little wonder that the various human-rights movements broke out on the college campuses in the sixties, for it is there on the megacampuses (mass education, mass enlightenment, is the grandest humanistic dream!), in the immense lecture halls, the closed-circuit television lectures, the turgid bureaucracies, that the loss of individual significance is felt in the very process of realizing the humanistic dream. Also, on the campuses it has become the growing belief that knowledge is not possible, that one system of thought is just as good as any other system of thought.

In order to comprise respectable, legitimate knowledge in the new humanistic world view, all things had to be conformable to the manipulations of man's autonomous reason. Speaking of the eighteenth century, the brilliant secular philosopher Ernst Cassirer says: "This philosophy believes in an original spontaneity of thought; it attributes to thought not merely an imitative function but the power and task of shaping life itself. Thought consists not only in analyzing and dissecting, but in actually bringing about that order of things which it conceives as necessary, so that by this act of fulfillment *it may demonstrate its own reality and truth.*"[3] Truth in an ultimate sense is not the philosophic goal for these thinkers; rather, the goal lies in the self-authentication of *the mind as the ultimate* creator and definer in the universe. Speaking further of reason as it serves the purpose of the new spirit, Cassirer says:

> What reason is, and what it can do, can never be known by its results but only by its function. And its most important function consists in its *power to bind and to dissolve. It dissolves everything merely factual, all simple data of experience, and everything believed on the evidence of revelation, tradition, and authority;* and it does not rest content until it has analyzed all these things into their simplest component parts and into their last elements of belief and opinion. Following this work of dissolution begins the work of construction. Reason cannot stop with the dispersed parts; *it has to build from them a new structure*, a true whole. But since reason creates this whole and fits the parts together according to its own rule, it gains complete knowledge of the structure of the product.[4]

Man's project is to re-create the universe in his own terms, independent of God and revelation, in order to assert the divinity of his thought. But the problems which have attended this project have been manifold, for man must find a way to account for what already has been given. As Rousas

Rushdoony and Cornelius Van Til have pointed out, the humanistic thinker must borrow presuppositions from the Judeo-Christian world view in order to conduct his thinking. He must begin his analysis of the world from the intelligent and dynamic patterns which God has created, then he must break these down in order to convert them into something of his own making. He also must begin with the assumption that the mind is suited for dealing with and understanding the world in which he finds himself. There is no guarantee for this except in Judeo-Christian terms.

So man finds himself in a form of intellectual schizophrenia, as seen clearly in someone like Hume. When God and his revelation are removed as the basis for order and clarity, there is no longer any objective, transcendent reference point which justifies the efforts of reason. These presuppositions of order and clarity have been slow in breaking down, but their collapse is ever more present in the twentieth century. Because this kind of secular thinking begins with the mind of man, the reality of the objective world comes more and more into question.

As we have seen, the result of Hume's analysis left man without possibility of significant knowledge, without self, in a world without substance or structure. The scientific community of his day was thrown into an uproar because, granted the premise (which they did not dispute), they could find no flaws in his thinking. Clearly, this was a problem, but how could it be resolved since reality is now an indeterminate philosophic entity which must be determined and defined by humanistic criteria? Given the age's program of capturing all things to the mind of man, Kant took the next logical step and attributed to mind the creative power which produces what we know as "reality." The implications of this step are enormous.

Kant developed his thought in two books which are worthy of note: *The Critique of Pure Reason* and *The Critique of Practical Reason*. In his *Critique of Pure Reason*, Kant sought to establish the authenticity of the scientific enterprise by describing the a priori activity of the mind mentioned above. In the *Critique of Practical Reason*, Kant sought to proclaim man's freedom as a religious and moral agent, but in a way which cut it off entirely from the sphere of intelligent reality, so that faith and knowledge stand in radical opposition. Kant placed God, soul, moral freedom, and the like in the realm of the unknowable "things in themselves." As things in themselves, they are to the knowing mind neither real nor unreal, neither living nor dead. Objective investigation, observation of the created cosmos, cannot even suggest probabilities for the existence of God, of immortality, for these in no way touch the reality which is ordered by the mind for experience. God has no inherent relation to human life as it can be known. He was making room for faith, Kant claimed, when he took this step, but he simultaneously caused faith to exist without reference to knowledge or intelligence. Neither occurrences in history nor the presence of life in a cosmos can provide justification for faith.

If one reasons earnestly about religious questions from such a philosophic position as Kant's, one can only arrive at an agonizing agnosticism because God has been structurally severed from any relationship to existence. If he exists, men, by definition, cannot know him. Proceeding from such assumptions, faith can only be a blind leap into the unknown. Faith can never be biblical faith, that is, trust based on evidence.[5]

APPENDIX TWO
THE WEST: THE POINT OF NO RETURN

For the time will come when they [men] will not endure sound doctrine; but wanting to have their ears tickled, they will accumulate for themselves teachers in accordance to their own desires; and will turn away their ears from the truth, and will turn aside to myths (2 Tim. 4:3, 4, NASB).

The remarkable developments in philosophy in the hundred years previous to Immanuel Kant found their culmination in him. Kant's influence on the modern world has been immense, and it is no exaggeration to say that he dominated the nineteenth century. (There have been those who argue that philosophically the nineteenth and twentieth centuries are footnotes to Kant.) His epistemology laid the groundwork for the new revolutionary spirit which swept the West in the form of Romanticism. The Romantics, the influential avant-garde thinkers, poets, and artists of the nineteenth century, felt the diminished portion of reality which was thereafter the antimetaphysical reductionism of the eighteenth century; its hard, natural determinism and its unfeeling, soulless universe impoverished man's vision of life. The Romantics did not question the humanistic and naturalistic assumptions of the Enlightenment; they merely sought to reverse the tendency toward impersonality by asserting the value or private experience over against mere scientific fact. More important than "objective" fact is the sensitive response of the individual. In this brief poem by Walt Whitman (1819-92) this tendency is most clearly seen.

> When I heard the learn'd astronomer,
> When the proofs, the figures, were
>   ranged in columns before me,
> When I was shown the charts and
>   diagrams, to add, divide,
>   and measure them,
> When I sitting heard the astronomer
>   where he lectured with much
>   applause in the lecture-room,
> How soon unaccountable I became
>   tired and sick,
> Till rising and gliding out I
>   wander'd off by myself,
> In the mystical moist night-air,
>   and from time to time,
> Look'd up in perfect silence at
>   the stars.

What matters for the Romantic is not the overwhelming accuracies of scientific knowledge, for these are dead facts; what matters is the living response—intuitive, moral, aesthetic, empathetic—of the private soul. One's sensitive feelings for objects of experience are the highest revelation.

    Kant's epistemology was adopted by the English Romantics through Coleridge and Carlyle and spread through them to America, where it was seized upon by influential writers like Thoreau, Emerson, and Whitman. The crucial importance of Kant resides in this: for him the creativity of the human mind was responsible for the form and structure of reality; by means of such a view, everything objective, everything outside man, was effectively neutered insofar as it might have a normative effect upon thinking and behavior. If mind is responsible for the structure of the world, if man is the creative source, then the world can be remade in conformity to man's desires, for reality is in itself formless and malleable. Thoreau was to assert in *Walden* that "The universe constantly and obediently answers to our conceptions .... Let us spend our lives in conceiving them." Man can create the universe he desires to live in simply by revolutionizing his thinking. As one of Oscar Wilde's paradoxes ran, art does not imitate nature; nature imitates art. The all-sufficient mind of man changes the world in conformity to his creative preoccupations. Reality becomes a kind of Rorschach blot, or a screen, which takes on the characteristics which the mind projects.

Another aspect of the Romantic project which found frequent expression was the occultic effort to penetrate to the secret world of "things in themselves." Many took the attitude (and still do) that since by definition the rational, causal structure of the world is an aspect of man's consciousness, the rational intelligence was an obstacle to true knowledge. Penetration to the true essence of things requires, then, deep intuition, mystical ecstasy, emotional transport, or some meditative or drug-induced trance. Ecstatic self-absorption into a mystical oneness with or through nature, most obvious in Wordsworth, Shelley, Whitman, becomes an almost conventional form of religious experience.

This tendency to regard nature as somehow divine and a place for mystical states was worked out in the nineteenth century to such a degree that it often wears the clothes of pantheism. So much was this the case that the first translation of Hindu and Buddhist texts made in that century had an immediate impact on Western minds. The timing was perfect, as exemplified by the thoughts of Arthur Schopenhauer, a German philosopher.

Schopenhauer began his thinking from the work of Kant, whom he admired greatly, and qualified it to be his own bitter and pessimistic view of life. In this way Schopenhauer arrived at a system of thought which amounts to a Western formulation of Buddhism. When he had contact with the sacred texts of Eastern occult practice, they merely confirmed what he had discovered by his own reflections and qualifications of Kant.

For Schopenhauer, the world men know is maya or illusion; the real reality he intuited behind life is a single, pervasive, and impersonal will which spawns this world of desire, suffering, boredom, and death. Schopenhauer believed that the only real escape from this prison house was the discipline of renunciation of the Buddhist, who extinguishes all desire to live and watches his body and mind waste away into nothingness.

Nineteenth-century French poet Arthur Rimbaud developed a theory of visionary poetry to enable him to penetrate phenomenal experience or maya by the systematic disordering of the senses. Thoreau also felt that men could penetrate maya to the reality behind appearance, though his vision was more optimistic. He used a Hindu anecdote in *Walden* to describe this occult potential in man:

> I have read a Hindoo book, that "there was a king's son, who, being expelled in infancy from the native city, was brought up by a forester, and, growing up to maturity in that state, imagined himself to belong to the barbarous race with which he lived. One of his father's ministers having discovered him, revealed to him what he was, and the misconception of his character was removed, and he knew himself to be a prince. So Soul," continues the Hindoo philosopher, "from the circumstances in which it is placed, mistakes its own character, until the truth is revealed to it by some holy teacher, and then it knows itself to be *Brahme* (God).[1]

Coupled with the movement into pantheism which the Romantic movement introduces from the Kantian epistemology is the effort to lay aside conceptions, both good and evil, as limitations upon human consciousness. Blake, the English mystic poet, called this project on which he was embarked the marriage of reason and hell. Later in the nineteenth century, the very terms *good* and *evil* were made irrelevant by persistent reductive analyses of experience. The most famous and influential of these came via the Englishman Walter Pater in the conclusion to his critical work, *The Renaissance*. Pater opened the door wide to the century's advancing interest in moral rebellion, perversion, mysticism, and occultism by abolishing truth for experience. "To regard all things and principles of things as inconstant modes or fashions has more and more become the tendency of modern thought," he says. Outwardly and inwardly, all we know is a passing world of impressions.

> Experience, already reduced to a group of impressions, is ringed round for each one of us by that thick wall of personality through which no real voice has ever pierced on its way to us, or from us to *that which we can only conjecture is without*. Every one of those impressions is the impression of the individual in his isolation, each mind keeping as a solitary prisoner its own dream of a world.[2]

So Pater asserts, as many in our day have, that "not the fruit of experience, but experience itself, is the end."[3] We should quicken ourselves by intensifying our experience. "To burn always with this hard, gem-like flame, to maintain this ecstasy, is success in life."[4]

Thought and theory do no more than screen our experiences; therefore, since experience itself is all we can know and enjoy, one must open up to all experiences, to all modes of being and behavior without exclusion. Moral questions are irrelevant, for as Pater goes on to say, "The theory or idea or system which requires of us the sacrifice of any part of this experience has no real claims upon us." Truth of any sort has no reference here, has no normative effect for Pater. Truth is not true but useful, as long as it serves our interests. Man's own experience is the god for whom all is sacrificed.

It is not surprising that the generations of avant-garde youth who followed Pater pursued all manner of experience, especially that which is strange, bizarre, and forbidden. Pater opened the door to all things, and so the art influenced by him became increasingly fantastic and occult, many artists exploring experience through drunkenness, addictions, séances, and black magic.

Pater's perception is not a passing one, and, strangely, there is always some inevitable connection between serious pursuit of the pleasure principle and the occult. Alan Watts, the late eclectic mystic who did much to popularize Zen in the West, presents a similar case for worship of openness and experience in many of his books, most notably in *Psychotherapy East and West*. Watts's humanistic analysis of experience results for him, as for Schopenhauer and others, in a metaphysical nihilism very close to that of the East. Life is no more than an interval of pulsating sensations; therefore, anything which enhances pleasure or reduces suffering is good. The appeal of Eastern pantheistic and nihilistic religions is, to one who has rejected the possibility of truth and knowledge in a meaningful sense, that they offer a developed philosophy and a way of life which directly aspires to suffusing one's life with occult power via meditation techniques and contact with spirit gods.

The noted semanticist, S. I. Hayakawa, former president of San Franciscio State and now a U. S. Senator, says that the universe is in perpetual flux. "The way that we happen to see and feel things is the result of the peculiarities of our nervous systems . . . . It is absurd, therefore, to imagine that we ever perceive anything 'as it really is.' "[5] "Things in themselves" are unknowable; truth is inaccessible and changing; what we "know" corresponds only to the limitations we bring to our experience. This is the root consciousness implicit in Kant's epistemology: Knowledge in any common sense of the word is problematic, for all we can know are mental constructs; and as far as ultimate significance is concerned, what we can know does not carry much weight.

This theory of knowledge has resulted in a despair in which humanism has been confronted with the bankruptcy of its own ill-fated project. If reality cannot be grasped in any meaningful sense, then what is the use? Gunther Stent, molecular biologist at the University of California at Berkeley, in his book, *The Coming of the Golden Age: A View of the End of Progress*, states that science is already on the decline because young students entering the sciences are no longer convinced that true knowledge is possible. Speaking as a secular observer, he feels that since God has been dethroned, there are no longer any clear-cut standards or values; and so feeling that correct discriminations are no longer possible with regard to human aspirations and behavior, the pleasure principle becomes the highest value in men's lives. The age of significant zealous research is behind us.[6]

Similarly, while an undergraduate, I encountered the same humanistic despair from one of the brightest minds I have ever met. When asked about the rationale for studying literary history, this English professor remarked, "It is an interesting way to pass the time, a creative way to deal with boredom." This intellectual despair is a growing phenomenon in the academy, the very seat of humanistic learning. Taking the place of the zeal for truth is the pursuit of self-satisfaction, a pursuit which, if taken seriously, leads into occultism, the pursuit of spiritual powers and pleasures, higher self-satisfactions.

A growing number of individuals in the West have sought to avoid humanistic desperation in the way the Romantics did—not by reexamining humanistic assumptions (indeed, they elaborate a religious faith upon the humanistic assertion of the ultimacy of the human mind), but by taking the problem of knowledge and using it as a springboard into mystery religion. This logic suggests that if the outer world is merely an aspect of my own mind, then real knowledge can be found within, in subjective experience. If the world men know is a function of limitations of the mind, then it requires only a small leap of faith to the belief that man can transcend these limitations through consciousness expansion. Indeed, Seth, the spirit guide for Jane Roberts, tells us that *"we form matter in order to operate in three-dimensional reality.... Physical matter is like plastic that we use to mold to our own desire."* When we recognize the limitations of three-dimensional reality, we can transcend it, ultimately becoming more spiritual, more powerful, and less physical by passing into the spirit world.

The Romantic movement was a consciousness-expanding movement which frequently sought revelation through drugs, love, mysticism, and the occult, as well as through arcane readings of the Bible and flirtation with magic. The Romantic doctrine of the creative imagination made man continuous with God, for it asserted that imagination made man continuous with God, for it asserted that imagination was a finite repetition of the infinite creative action of God. Therefore, man could expand Godward.

In the twentieth century, Henry Miller has sought an

expanded reality through astrology, mysticism, and sex. At the height of the nineteenth century, Whitman said in "Song of Myself":

> Divine am I inside and out, and
>   I make holy whatever I touch
>   or am touched from,
> The scent of these arm-pits aroma
>   finer than prayer,
> This head more than churches,
>   Bibles, and all the creeds.

And Miller, Whitman's modern literary successor, states in *Tropic of Capricorn* that his "whole aim in life is to get near to God, that is, to get nearer to myself."

The world of humanistic rationality is at a dead end, as modern observers have continued to point out, for without God, nothing, not even knowledge, is guaranteed. Taking off from the dead end in which humanism finds itself, the new occultists assert that reason must be left behind for higher, more inward, ways of "knowing." We must, they tell us, let go of our limited conception of God and an objective physical universe and recognize that they, too, are part of the vast evolving universal consciousness of which God is an idea. This is, in fact, pantheism, the perennial religion of fallen man who wishes to denature a wholly transcendent God and assert his own divinity. "The answer is within you," spiritist Elisabeth Kubler-Ross tells us. "Death can show us the way." And we, too, can "live each day as if it were the only one we had." Like the suicidal poet and mystic Shelley, who said, "Life, like a dome of many-colored glass,/Stains the white radiance of Eternity," Kubler-Ross says, "Death . . . may be viewed as the curtain between the existence that we are conscious of and one that is hidden from us until we raise that curtain."

Greater numbers of scientific researchers and the lay public alike seem willing to accept the spiritism, the astral projection, and occult philosophy offered by Raymond Moody and Kubler-Ross because the West has lived for two centuries with an epistemology which negates the God of

THE WEST: THE POINT OF NO RETURN

Scripture, while lending weight to man's pantheistic tendency. (Talk to plants, we are told.) With chilling arrogance and condescension, the Judeo-Christian God, the sovereign Father of creation, is dismissed as a symbol of unenlightened man's limited hopes and fears, as an archaic hangover from an ignorant, patriarchal period in man's adolescence. With the same breath we are encouraged to take hope in the secret and unexplored regions of consciousness, in messages from the "other side." Clearly, the "enlightened" mind believes that any God who exists must be either a positive life-force, which pulsates the universe with good vibrations, or some infinite benign, infinitely evolved, spirit who operates in terms of the generous wisdom of Dr. Benjamin Spock. He is there, patiently waiting for us to join him at his own level of being.

Having consciously bled the biblical God from his thinking about the universe, man has been faced with a spiritual and intellectual crisis, which he has sought to meet in desperate ways. Modern man finds himself trapped within the mind which the Enlightenment claimed was salvation. When secular reason based on sense experience cannot discover the truth about the universe, man will not turn back in repentance to the God he has denied; instead, he will interest himself in extrasensory perception, in extraterrestrial intelligence, out-of-the-body travel, in all forms of the occult. The occult promise is one of power to an impotent mind-power, at least, to transcend the laws of physical nature and transcend the humbling conclusions to which his reason brought him.

The times are ripe for curious-minded scientific dabbling in the occult; modern philosophy in the past two hundred years has paved the way. Moody and Kubler-Ross have appeared at a time when moral and spiritual confusion is so great that the only response of the "enlightened" to the conflicting claims of various beliefs has been to preach openness and tolerance. Rejecting the revelation of God, the intelligent man has no standard, no basis in truth, from which to make intelligent moral and religious discriminations. Tolerance has become the only way of dealing with conflicting, even contradictory, world views. Each is viewed as being equally valid and as a matter of mere private opinion. But as philosopher E. M. Adams has pointed out, tolerance may be no more than the "product of indifference, of the conviction that nothing really matters, that everything goes, that everything is permitted."[7] Such an attitude reflects a widespread loss of values, a moral and intellectual impotence which breeds an environment of dilettantes, of men who pursue ideas, philosophies, religious practices, not for truth value, but for gratification of their egos. Kubler-Ross and Moody fit well into this scheme of things because they offer a philosophy which tickles the fancies of men. As G. K. Chesterton said, when men give up their belief in God, "they do not believe in nothing; they believe in anything."

APPENDIX THREE
OLD TESTAMENT PREDICTIONS WHICH WERE LITERALLY FULFILLED IN CHRIST[1]

Floyd Hamilton in *The Basis of Christian Faith* (a modern defense of the Christian religion, revised and enlarged edition; New York, Harper and Row, 1964, p. 160) says that: "Canon Liddon is an authority for the statement that there are in the Old Testament 332 distinct predictions which were literally fulfilled in Christ."

1. His First Advent 29/
   The Fact. Gen 3:15; Deut. 18:15; Ps. 89:20; Isa. 9:6; 28:16; 32:1; 35:4; 42:6; 49:1; 55:4; Ezek. 34:24; Dan. 2:44; Mic. 4:1; Zech. 3:8.
   The Time. Gen. 49:10; Num. 24:17; Dan. 9:24; Mal. 3:1.
   His Divinity. Ps. 2:7, 11; 45:6, 7, 11; 72:8; 102:24-27; 89:26, 27; 110:1; Isa. 9:6; 25:9; 40:10; Jer. 23:6; Mic. 5:2; Mal. 3:1.
   Human Generation. Gen. 12:3; 18:18; 21:12; 22:18; 26:4; 28:14; 49:10; 2 Sam. 7:14; Ps. 18:4-6, 50; 22:22, 23; 89:4; 29:36; 132:11; Isa. 11:1; Jer. 23:5; 33:15.
2. His Forerunner
   Isa. 40:3; Mal. 3:1; 4:5.
3. His Nativity and Early Years
   The Fact. Gen. 3:15; Isa. 7:14; Jer. 31:22.
   The Place. Num. 24:17, 19; Mic. 5:2.
   Adoration by Magi. Ps. 72:10, 15; Isa. 60:3, 6.
   Descent into Egypt. Hos. 11:1
   Massacre of Innocents. Jer. 31:15.

4. His Mission and Office
   Mission. Gen. 12:3; 49:10; Num. 24:19; Deut. 18:18, 19; Ps. 21:1; Isa. 59:20; Jer. 33:16.
   Priest like Melchizedek. Ps. 110:4.
   Prophet like Moses. Deut. 18:15.
   Conversion of Gentiles. Isa. 11:10; Deut. 32:43; Ps. 18:49; 19:4; 117:1; Isa. 42:1; 45:23; 49:6; Hos. 1:10; 2:23; Joel 2:32.
   Galilee, Ministry in. Isa. 9:1, 2.
   Miracles. Isa. 35:5, 6; 42:7; 53:4.
   Spiritual graces. Ps. 45:7; Isa. 11:2; 42:1; 53:9; 61:1, 2.
   Preaching. Ps. 2:7; 78:2; Isa. 2:3; 61:1; Mic. 4:2.
   Purification of Temple. Ps. 61:9.
5. His Passion
   Rejection by Jews and Gentiles. Ps. 2:1; 22:12; 41:5; 56:5; 69:8; 118:22, 23; Isa. 6:9, 10; 8:14; 29:13; 53:1; 65:2.
   Persecution. Ps. 22:6; 35:7, 12; 56: 5; 71:10; 109:2; Isa. 49:7; 53:3.
   Triumphal Entry into Jerusalem. Ps. 8:2; 118:25, 26; Zech. 9:9.
   Betrayal by Own Friend. Ps. 41:9; 55:13; Zech. 13:6.
   Betrayal for Thirty Pieces. Zech. 11:12.
   Betrayer's Death. Ps. 55:15, 23; 109:17.
   Purchase of Potter's Field. Zech. 11:13.
   Desertion by Disciples. Zech. 13:7.
   False Accusation. Ps. 27:12; 35:11; 109:2; Ps. 2:1, 2.
   Silence under Accusation. Ps. 38:13; Isa. 53:7.
   Mocking. Ps. 22:7, 8, 16; 109:25.
   Insult, Buffeting, Spitting, Scourging. Ps. 35:15, 21; Isa. 50:6.
   Patience under Suffering. Isa. 53:7-9.
   Crucifixion. Ps. 22:14, 17.
   Gall and Vinegar, Offer of. Ps. 69:21.
   Prayer for Enemies. Ps. 109:4.
   Cries upon the Cross. Ps. 22:1; 31:5.
   Death in Prime of Life. Ps. 89:45; 102:24.
   Death with Malefactors. Isa. 53:9, 12.
   Death Attested by Convulsions of Nature. Amos 5:20; Zech. 14:4, 6.
   Casting Lots for Vesture. Ps. 22:18.
   Bone Not to Be Broken. Ps. 34:20.

Piercing. Ps. 22:16; Zech. 12:10; 13:6.
Voluntary death. Ps. 40:6-8.
Vicarious Suffering. Isa. 53:4-6, 12; Dan. 9:26.
Burial with the Rich. Isa. 53:9.
6. His Resurrection
Ps. 16:8-10; 30:3; 41:10; 118:17; Hos. 6:2.
7. His Ascension
Ps. 16:11; 24:7; 68:18; 110:1; 118:19.
8. His Second Advent
Ps. 50:3-6; Isa. 9:6, 7; 66:18; Dan. 7:13, 14; Zech. 12:10; 14:4-8.
Dominion Universal and Everlasting. I Chron. 17:11-14; Ps. 72:8; Isa. 9:7; Dan. 7:14; Ps. 2:6-8; 8:6; 110:1-3; 45:6, 7.

PROPHECIES FULFILLED CONFIRMS JESUS AS THE MESSIAH, THE CHRIST, THE SON OF GOD[2]

1. Objection: Fulfilled Prophecy in Jesus Was Deliberate
   Answer: The above objection might seem plausible until we realize that many of the prophecies concerning the Messiah were totally beyond the human control of Jesus, such as—
   1. Place of birth (Micah 5:2).
   2. Time of birth (Daniel 9:25; Genesis 49:10).
   3. Manner of birth (Isaiah 7:14).
   4. Betrayal.
   5. Manner of death (Psalm 22:16).
   6. People's reactions (mocking, spitting, staring, etc.).
   7. Piercing.
   8. Burial.
2. Objection: Fulfilled Prophecy in Jesus Was Coincidental, an Accident
   "Why, you could find some of these prophecies fulfilled in Kennedy, King, Nasser, etc.," replies the critic.

Answer: Yes, one could possibly find one or two prophecies fulfilled in other men, but not all 60 major prophecies! In fact, if you can find someone, other than Jesus, either living or dead, who can fulfill only half of the predictions concerning Messiah which are given in *Messiah in Both Testaments*, by

Fred John Meldau, the Christian Victory Publishing Company of Denver is ready to give you a $1,000 reward. There are a lot of men in the universities that could use some extra cash!

H. Harold Hartzler, of the American Scientific Affiliation, Goshen College, in the foreword of Stoner's book writes that, "The manuscript for *Science Speaks* has been carefully reviewed by a committee of the American Scientific Affiliation members and by the Executive Council of the same group and has been found, in general, to be dependable and accurate in regard to the scientific material presented. The mathematical analysis included is based upon principles of probability which are thoroughly sound and Professor Stoner has applied these principles in a proper and convincing way."

The following probabilities are taken from Peter Stoner in *Science Speaks* (Moody Press, 1963) to show that coincidence is ruled out by the science of probability. Stoner says that by using the modern science of probability in reference to eight prophecies (1.—No. 10; 2.—No. 22; 3.—No. 27; 4.—No. 33 and 44; 5.—No. 34; 6.—No. 35 and 36; 7.—No. 39; 8.—No. 44 and 45 [crucified]) "we find that the chance that any man might have lived down to the present time and fulfilled all eight prophecies is 1 in 10^{17}." That would be 1 in 100,000,000,000,000,000. In order to help us comprehend this staggering probability, Stoner illustrates it by supposing that "we take 10^{17} silver dollars and lay them on the face of Texas. They will cover all of the state two feet deep. Now mark one of these silver dollars and stir the whole mass thoroughly, all over the state. Blindfold a man and tell him that he can travel as far as he wishes, but he must pick up one silver dollar and say that this is the right one. What chance would he have of getting the right one? Just the same chance that the prophets would have had of writing these eight prophecies and having them all come true in any one man, from their day to the present time, providing they wrote them in their own wisdom.

"Now these prophecies were either given by inspiration of God or the prophets just wrote them as they thought they should be. In such a case the prophets had just one chance in 10^{17} of having them come true in any man, but they all came true in Christ.

"This means that the fulfillment of these eight prophecies alone proves that God inspired the writing of those prophecies to a definiteness which lacks only one chance in 10^{17} of being absolute." 24/100-107

Stoner considers 48 prophecies and says, "we find the chance that any one man fulfilled all 48 prophecies to be 1 in 10^{157}.

"This is really a large number and it represents an extremely small chance. Let us try to visualize it. The silver dollar, which we have been using, is entirely too large. We must select a smaller object. The electron is about as small an object as we know of. It is so small that it will take 2.5 times 10^{15} of them laid side by side to make a line, single file, one inch long. If we were going to count the electrons in this line one inch long, and counted 250 each minute, and if we counted day and night, it would take us 19,000,000 years to count just the one-inch line of electrons. If we had a cubic inch of these electrons and we tried to count them it would take us, counting steadily 250 each minute, 19,000,000 times 19,000,000 times 19,000,000 years or 6.9 times 10^{21} years.

"With this instruction, let us go back to our chance of 1 in 10^{157}. Let us suppose that we are taking this number of electrons, marking one, and thoroughly stirring it into the whole mass, then blindfolding a man and letting him try to find the right one. What chance has he of finding the right one? What kind of a pile will this number of electrons make? They make an inconceivably large volume." 24/109, 110

Such is the chance of any one man fulfilling 48 prophecies.

FOR FURTHER READING

I. Evidence for the Truth of Christianity (Apologetics)
Henry, Carl. *God, Revelation, and Authority.* Waco, Tex.: Word, 1977.
Lewis, C. S. *Mere Christianity.* London: Fontana, 1952.
Lewis, Gordon. *Testing Christianity's Truth Claims.* Chicago: Moody, 1976.
McDowell, Josh. *Evidence That Demands a Verdict.* Arrowhead Springs, San Bernadino, Calif.: Campus Crusade, 1972.
Pinnock, Clark. *Set Forth Your Case.* Chicago: Moody, 1971.
Smith, Wilbur. *Therefore Stand.* Grand Rapids: Baker, 1969.

II. Christianity and Western Civilization
Guinness, Os. *The Dust of Death.* Downers Grove, Ill.: Inter-Varsity, 1973.
Montgomery, John Warwick. *Where Is History Going?* Minneapolis: Bethany Fellowship, 1974.
Rushdoony, Rousas. *The One and the Many.* Nutley, N. J.: Craig, 1971.
Schaeffer, Francis. *The God Who Is There.* Downers Grove, Ill.: Inter-Varsity, 1968.
_____. *How Should We Then Live?* Old Tappan, N. J.: Revell, 1977.

FOR FURTHER READING

III. The True Christian Message

Lewis, C. S. *Mere Christianity*. London: Fontana, 1952.

Packer, J. I. *Knowing God*. Downers Grove, Ill.: Inter-Varsity, 1974.

Stott, John. *Basic Christianity*. Downers Grove, Ill.: Inter-Varsity, 1971.

NOTES

Chapter 2
1. Raymond A. Moody, Jr., *Life After Life* (Covington, Ga.: Mockingbird Books, 1975), p. 9. Used by permission. Copyright © Mockingbird Books, Covington, Ga., 1975. All rights reserved.
2. Ibid., p. 23.
3. Ibid., p. 79.
4. Ibid., p. 84.

Chapter 3
1. John Weldon and Zola Levitt, *Is There Life After Death?* (Irvine, Calif.: Harvest House, 1977), p. 32.
2. Ibid.
3. Ibid., p. 37.
4. Ibid., p. 38.
5. Raymond A. Moody, Jr., *Life After Life* (Covington, Ga.: Mockingbird Books, 1975), p. 103.
6. Elisabeth Kubler-Ross, interview in *National Enquirer* (Feb. 1, 1977).
7. *Deccan Herald* (Dehli, India, Oct. 26, 1977).

Chapter 4
1. Thomas Sugrue, *There Is A River* (New York: Holt, Rinehart & Winston, 1942), p. 361.
2. Ford also gave Sun Myung Moon, head of the Unification Church, a number of séances. On May 13, 1964, Ford's spirit guide, Fletcher, said of Moon, "He is a child of the new age—the Aquarian age. He has tremendous spiritual power and also psychic power . . . he is a prophet" (Allen Spraggett, *Arthur Ford: The Man Who Talked with the Dead* [New York: Signet Books, 1974], p. 271). Copyright © 1973 by Allen Spraggett. Reprinted by arrangement with The New American Library, Inc., New York, N.Y.
3. Joseph Bayly, *What About Horoscopes?* (Elgin, Ill.: D.C. Cook, 1970), p. 63.
4. Spraggett, p. 25.

NOTES

5. Ibid., p. 41.
6. Ibid., pp. 130-31.
7. Ibid., p. 125.
8. Elisabeth Kubler-Ross, interview in the *National Enquirer* (Feb. 1, 1977).
9. Spraggett, p. 270.
10. Raphael Gasson, *The Challenging Counterfeit* (Plainfield, N.J.: Logos, 1966), p. 48.
11. Spraggett, p. 210.
12. Gasson, p. 54. (The identical beliefs come through Moody's editorializing; see p. 70 of his book.)
13. Ibid., p. 119.
14. Ibid.

Chapter 5
1. James Pearre, interview with Elisabeth Kubler-Ross, *San Francisco Examiner and Chronicle*, Nov. 14, 1976. Reprinted, courtesy of *The Chicago Tribune*.
2. Raymond Moody, *Life After Life* (Covington, Ga.: Mockingbird Books, 1975), pp. 72-73.
3. Ibid., p. 45.
4. Ibid., p. 66.
5. Ibid., p. 70.
6. Ibid.
7. Ibid.
8. Ibid., italics added.
9. Jane Roberts, *Seth Speaks* (New York: Bantam Books, 1973).
10. Jane Roberts, *The Seth Material* (New York: Bantam Books, 1970).

Chapter 6
1. C.S. Lewis, *Miracles* (New York: Macmillan, 1947), pp. 84-85.
2. Erwin Schrodinger, *My View of the World* (London: Cambridge U. Press, 1964), p. 67.
3. That such a created substrate has existed seems a reasonable inference from the account of Genesis 1:1-10, where it is revealed that the initial stage of cosmic formation was a state which possessed true created existence, but was "formless and void." It was only later that this unitary state of bare existence was molded by God to pass through the primordial duality (the separation of light and darkness, v. 4) and beyond into increasingly elaborate dualizations (separation of firmaments, land from water, etc., vv. 6-27) by means of which God built up the complex forms of material creation.

Chapter 7
1. Tal Brooke, *The Amazing Advent* (New Delhi: Nabajiban Press, 1971).
2. *The Bhagavad Gita*, 7:14.
3. Ibid., 8:6.
4. Ibid., 8:9, 10.
5. Tal Brooke, "Lord of the Air," manuscript.

Chapter 8
1. Elisabeth Kubler-Ross, *Death: The Final State of Growth* (Englewood Cliffs, N.J.: Prentice-Hall, 1975), pp. 1-3. © 1975. Reprinted by permission of Prentice-Hall, Inc., Englewood Cliffs, N.J.

2. Brooks Alexander, "The Coming World Religion," an essay published by Spiritual Counterfeits Projects, Inc., Berkeley, CA. Used by permission.
3. Alexander Hislop, *The Two Babylons* (Neptune, N.J.: Loiseaux, 1916), pp. 20, 78, 96, italics added.
4. Manglwadi, *The World of Gurus* (New Delhi: Vikas Publishing, 1977), p. 174, italics added.
5. Kubler-Ross, pp. 164-67, italics added.
6. Lennie Kronish, "Elisabeth Kubler-Ross: Messenger of Love," *Yoga Journal* (Nov.-Dec. 1976).

Chapter 9
1. *The Daily Progress* (Nov. 25, 1977), Charlottesville, Virginia.
2. For a more thorough analysis of the historical progression, refer to the Appendixes by Robert Schlagal.

Chapter 10
1. C.S. Lewis, *Mere Christianity* (New York: Macmillan, 1952), p. 32.
2. Malcolm Muggeridge, as quoted in *Eternity* (April 1972).

Chapter 11
1. F.F. Bruce, *The Books and the Parchments* (Old Tappan, N.J.: Revell, 1963), p. 88. Used by permission.
2. Josh McDowell, *Evidence That Demands a Verdict* (Arrowhead Springs, San Bernadino, Calif.: Campus Crusade, 1972), p. 19. Used by permission.
3. Reprinted by Baker Book House, Grand Rapids, 1965.
4. J.N.D. Anderson, "The Resurrection of Jesus Christ," *Christianity Today* (March 29, 1968).
5. A.T. Robertson, as quoted by McDowell, p. 46.
6. Sir Frederic G. Kenyon, as quoted by McDowell, p. 47.
7. McDowell, p. 150.
8. Norman L. Geisler and William E. Nix, *A General Introduction to the Bible* (Chicago: Moody, 1968), p. 263.
9. Clark Pinnock, *Set Forth Your Case* (Chicago: Moody, 1971), p. 86.
10. C.S. Lewis, *Mere Christianity* (New York: Macmillan, 1952), p. 40.

Chapter 12
1. C.S. Lewis, *Screwtape Proposes a Toast* (London: Collins, 1965), p. 109.
2. *The Westminster Confession*, chap. 32.
3. Ibid., chap. 33.
4. Louis Berkhof, *Systematic Theology* (Grand Rapids: Eerdmans, 1941), p. 259. Used by permission.
5. Ibid., p. 261.
6. E.W. Hengstenburg, *The Christology of the Old Testament* (Grand Rapids: Kregel, 1970).
7. See James Strong, *The Exhaustive Concordance of the Bible* (New York: Abingdon, 1958 reprint).

Conclusion
1. Malachi Martin, *Hostage to the Devil* (New York: Bantam Books, 1977).

Appendix 1
1. William Barrett, *Irrational Man* (Garden City, N.Y.: Doubleday, Anchor Books, 1958), pp. 216-17.

NOTES

2. Ibid., p. 217.
3. Ernst Cassirer, *The Philosophy of the Enlightenment* (Princeton, N.J.: Princeton U. Press, 1951), pp. 13, 14, italics added.
4. Ibid.
5. The thinking of Kant quite naturally led to Kierkegaard and from there to modern existential theology, in terms of which God is not an active, intelligent, and sovereign Lord, but a creative life force, a symbol of wholeness or resolution, or a value-producing agent which can only be encountered inwardly in subjective experience. For all intents and purposes in this camp, the God of Scripture is dead.

Appendix 2
1. Henry Thoreau, *Walden* (New York: New American Library, Signet Classic, 1960), p. 67.
2. Walter Pater, *The Renaissance* (New York: Mentor Books, 1977), p. 156.
3. Ibid., p. 157.
4. Ibid., p. 158.
5. S.I. Hayakawa, article in *Aspects of Composition*, edited by Billie A. Inman and Ruth Gardner (New York: Harcourt, Brace & World, 1967), p. 33.
6. Gunther Stent, *The Coming of the Golden Age: A View of the End of Progress* (Garden City, N.Y.: Natural History Press, 1969).
7. E.M. Adams, "A Changing America: Morale and Morality," an essay.

Appendix 3
1. Quoted from Josh McDowell, *Evidence That Demands a Verdict* (Arrowhead Springs, San Bernadino, Calif.: Campus Crusade, 1971), pp. 181-83. Printed by permission. Copyright © Campus Crusade for Christ, Inc., 1971. All rights reserved.
2. Quoted from ibid., pp. 174-76. Printed by permission.